ASKING
QUESTIONS

A Classroom Model for Teaching the Bible

D. Bruce Lockerbie

What Does It Say?

What Does It Mean?

How Does This Apply to Me?

*They read from the Book of the Law of God,
making it clear and giving the meaning so that the
people could understand what was being read.*

Nehemiah 8:8, NIV

*There are two things necessary to the treatment of
the Scriptures: a way of discovering those things
which are to be understood, and a way of teaching
what we have learned.*

St. Augustine
On Christian Doctrine

*True discernment in the interpretation of God's
Word is in direct ratio to the prayerfulness of the
interpreter.*

Frank E. Gaebelein
Exploring the Bible

ASKING QUESTIONS

A Classroom Model
for Teaching the Bible

D. Bruce Lockerbie

Mott Media
Milford, Michigan

ACKNOWLEDGMENTS

Unless otherwise identified, quotations from the Bible are taken from *Holy Bible: New International Version*. Copyright © 1978 by the New York International Bible Society. Used by permission of Zondervan Bible Publishers. However, neither the method of study nor the lesson material in this book depends upon any single translation. In preparing this book, for instance, I have compared several translations and paraphrases, including King James Version (KJV), Revised Standard Version (RSV), New English Bible (NEB), Phillips, Today's English Version (TEV), and Living Bible (LB).

Library of Congress Cataloging in Publication Data

Lockerbie, D   Bruce.
    Asking questions.

    Bibliography: p.
    1. Bible—Study.   2.   Bible—Study—Outlines, syllabi, etc.   I.   Title.
    BS600.2.L55   220'.07   80-18198
    ISBN 0-915134-75-6 (pbk.)

To my sister Jeannie,
a Bible teacher
in Bangladesh

CONTENTS

PREFACE

When I was a child, I once won a week's vacation at a summer camp on the strength of knowing that Daniel's Babylonian name was Belteshazzar. Of course, I had to know a little more than that along the way, but it was this final bit of information that got me the free week at camp.

I'm not, however, a Bible scholar and don't pretend to be. My academic training is in rhetoric and literature; my professional experience classifies me as a writer and teacher of literature and other arts. But for a quarter-century I've also been teaching the Bible—in secondary school classrooms, in Sunday schools and youth groups, to teenagers on weekend retreats, to adults at conferences, to college students and missionaries, to seminarians and pastors.

Much of what I know about the Bible—including the obscure names of biblical characters—I learned at home, where one of our family entertainments was quizzing at mealtime. In Sunday school my teachers seldom had the attractive materials now available from commercial publishers; they had to improvise and catch their students' interest by storytelling, and so I learned from them. At weekly children's meetings we sang songs such as "Let us sing the Books of Moses, of Moses, of Moses...." To this day, when I'm leafing through the Old Testament, that song reminds me that the Book of Joel is just before Amos, just after Hosea. At these meetings, as well as at Vacation Bible School, we had stories illustrated first by old-fashioned lantern slides, then by an amazing new visual aid called flannelgraph. We played "Sword Drill" and "Bible Baseball" and "Twenty Questions"—all corny and hokey and terribly competitive; and, I might add, all terribly effective at imparting a basic knowledge of Bible stories.

But, perhaps like you, I had no formal Bible college or seminary courses in how to teach the Bible in a school setting. Most of what I've learned, therefore, about teaching the Bible has come from on-the-job training—from colleagues at The Stony Brook School with whom I've shared my questions; from pupils whose own questions have often cut through any of my supposed knowledge to reach the very heart of the matter. To all of them, my gratitude for what they have taught me.

This book tries to bring together some of what I've learned in teaching Bible classes to boys and girls in grades 7–12. Its main purpose is to help school teachers of the Bible to develop into confident guides and mentors as they lead their pupils in studying God's Word.

I wish to thank Robert E. Gustafson, Jr., chairman of the Bible department, The Stony Brook School, for reading this manuscript with a discerning eye. I must also thank my editor, Diane Zimmerman, for her encouragement and Mary Rost, my typist, for her unfailing reliability.

I would like to hear from you. If you have any questions about this method of Bible teaching, please write. Share with me your successes and insights.

D. Bruce Lockerbie
Dean of Faculty
The Stony Brook School
Chapman Parkway
Stony Brook, NY 11790

D.B.L.
July 1980

INTRODUCTION

God's Revelation of Himself

God the Father's greatest gift to the creature made in his image is his revelation of himself to human beings. By his grace God makes it possible for us to know him by name and call him Father. Throughout the pagan world one of the tragedies of heathen religion is that the deity to be worshiped either can't be known at all or must be recognized in some dreadful shape and grotesque manifestation. Not so with God the Father Almighty, Maker of heaven and earth. He is Jehovah, the Lord of hosts, the God of Abraham, Isaac, and Jacob, the Ancient of Days; above all else, he is the *God-who-is*, actively and unceasingly caring for his Creation.

God makes himself known to us in various ways. Paul demonstrates in Romans 1 and 2 that God's presence in the universe ought to be apparent to anyone who can perceive order in nature, anyone who can recognize the human capacity for common decency. But contrary to the cynicism of Ezra Pound's "Ballad for Gloom," our God is not "a gallant foe that playeth behind the veil." Instead, he is the God who chooses to step across the chasm separating eternity from time and celestial glory from mundaneness. He chooses to disclose himself as one of us in the person of Jesus of Nazareth, accepting full responsibility for what it means to be human—the peculiarity of our birth, the helplessness of our infancy, the pangs of hunger and fatigue, of disappointment and betrayal, as well as the utter loneliness of death. In his humiliation, God allows himself no special privileges; his only reservation is that through it all Jesus of Nazareth should be free from sin. In every other respect he becomes at one and the same time wholly God and wholly man. He is exactly who the apostle Peter calls him, "the Christ, the Son of the living God," the supreme revelation of God to the human race. Jesus is no mere avatar, such as Hindus recognize in their holy men; he is no mere apotheosis of the divine in man, such as the Greeks honored in Heracles, Achilles, or their other superheroes. Jesus of Nazareth is a singular, unique embodying of God-in-man, the promise of Emmanuel or "God-with-us" completely fulfilled. This, then, is the mystery of the Incarnation:

> The Word now dwells among us,
> Made flesh, yet very God.

But like any other historical event, the unique appearing of God in human form flashes through time like a meteor. Its wonder and significance would be lost to later generations were it not for the written record preserved for us in the Bible. Through God's grace human beings whose lifespan falls two thousand years after the Incarnation can nonetheless participate by faith in the reality of "God-with-us" through reading the Gospel accounts of the life and work of Jesus of Nazareth and thereafter believing what the Gospels say. Furthermore, we can trace all of God's dealings with humanity, from Creation to the anticipated Consummation of the Ages, by reading and studying the pages of Holy Scripture. While we must never discount the mystery of the Word-becoming-flesh, in a certain reverent sense it's true to say that the Incarnation would have been an event of limited importance had it not also been true that the Word became language and literature, thus making its meaning available to us.

Some people who merely admire the person of Jesus of Nazareth discredit the Bible's claims. But is it possible to have it both ways? This becomes the critical issue for all Christians. The Bible is uniquely the Word of God, his verbal revelation; the Bible is also the one sure way by which we may come to know who God the Father is, that Jesus of Nazareth is his Son, that the Holy Spirit lives in those who believe, what our purpose is in living, what our eternal destiny will be. There is no such thing as living by the example of Jesus while at the same time ignoring the source of whatever knowledge we have of that example. The Bible alone gives firsthand historical evidence; any other source of information is hearsay. That is why the apostle John says over and over again, "I write this to you so that . . . ." or "I write to you because . . . ." His authority for writing at all comes from his being an eyewitness; John is emphatic as he says, "We repeat, we really saw and heard what we are writing to you about" (1 John 1:3, Phillips).

From the time of Moses through the period of the church fathers who fixed the canon of Scripture, both Jews and Christians relied on the written Word of God for precept and example. Moses descended from the mountain with shining face, but he also bore the tablets inscribed by the finger of God. Pagan priests may have examined the entrails of sacrificial animals, but the ancient prophet's testimony was always, "Thus says the Lord!" Jesus himself referred often to the sacred writings familiar to his listeners, the Law and the Prophets. We too must be people of the Book. As Richard France, Warden of Tyndale House, Cambridge, England, has written in his article, "Jesus Christ and the Bible" in *Eerdmans' Handbook to the Bible:*

> As a Christian I want to follow Jesus Christ. I want to do what he said, go where he leads, follow his example, enter into the life he offers . . . . So I seek the authority of Jesus; and I am led on by him to see the authority of the Bible. We cannot have one without the other (p. 37).

Robert E. Webber, in *Common Roots,* reminds us that "the Old Testament Scriptures were regarded as the Scriptures of the New Testament church because the apostles had received this precedent from Jesus" (Grand Rapids: Zondervan, 1978, p. 121). But even as early as the latter half of the first century, when evangelists and apostles were composing those narratives and letters which were to become the New Testament, they understood the importance of their written accounts of Jesus' life and written admonitions to the early church. Luke specifically uses the language of a legal affidavit to insist upon the veracity and accuracy of his Gospel. He has taken the testimony of eyewitnesses, he says, and has "carefully investigated everything from the beginning" (Luke 1:3, NIV) in order to write "an orderly account" ("a connected narrative," says the NEB). His purpose, he tells Theophilus, is "so that you may know the certainty of

the things you have been taught" (Luke 1:4, NIV). The apostle
Paul claims, in several of his letters, to be writing under the
power of the Holy Spirit; for instance, he tells the Corinthians,
"This is what we speak, not in words taught us by human wisdom but in words taught by the Spirit, expressing spiritual
truths in spiritual words" (1 Cor. 2:13, NIV). Consequently, Paul
is competent to determine the spiritual maturity and integrity of
a person precisely by how well anyone recognizes Paul's authority in writing as he does: "If anybody thinks he is a prophet
or spiritually gifted, let him acknowledge that what I am writing
to you is the Lord's command" (1 Cor. 14:37, NIV). And Peter
also corroborates Paul's claim by classifying Paul's letters (difficult as some of them are to understand, Peter agrees!) with "the
other Scriptures" (2 Peter 3:15–16, NIV).

The place of the written Word in the writings of the church
fathers shows with what authority it was regarded. By the end of
the second century, the widely scattered church was formulat-
ing its creeds and rules of faith to express its common beliefs.
Throughout these declarations of faith called *symbols*—the
Latin word for "passport," recognizing someone's citizenship, is
the word used—numerous quotations from the New Testament
appear. For instance, writing around A.D. 190, Irenaeus quotes
from Philippians 2:10–11 in his rule of faith. Two centuries
later, John Chrysostom advises his audience to find comfort in
times of grief from the New Testament Scriptures, "the oracles
of God," in these dramatic words: "Dive into them as into a
chest of medicines" (Homily IX, on Colossians 3:16,17). He
further goes on to say that "not knowing the Scriptures" is "the
cause of all evils."

One of the beautiful prayers in *The Book of Common Prayer*
summons us to this same kind of deep experience with the
Word of God:

> Blessed Lord, who hast caused all holy Scriptures to be written for
> our learning; Grant that we may in such wise hear them, read,
> mark, learn, and inwardly digest them, that by patience and com-
> fort of thy holy Word, we may embrace, and ever hold fast, the
> blessed hope of everlasting life, which thou hast given us in our
> Saviour Jesus Christ. Amen.

"All Scripture is God-breathed," Paul tells Timothy, "and is useful for teaching, rebuking, correcting and training in right-eousness, so that the man of God may be thoroughly equipped for every good work" (2 Tim. 3:16-17, NIV). Notice the parallels between Paul's description of the usefulness of Scripture and the words of the prayer: *read, mark, learn, and inwardly digest.*

Simply reading the Bible, essential as that is, can never be enough for the Christian who wants to know as much as possible of God's Word. He must "dive" into it, as Chrysostom urges. This means much more than the parody of Bible reading cari-catured by the person who shuts his eyes, flips open the book, and runs his finger down the page to find a verse for the day. It also means more than taking snatches out of context from some compendium such as *Daily Light.* To know the Bible one must study the Bible, the way an astronomer studies the sky or a gem expert examines a precious jewel. But before we can study an expanse of sky or a fragment of crystal, we must learn what we're looking for and how to find it.

PART ONE

Principles of the
Question and Answer Method

CHAPTER 1

The Gift of Teaching

So you've just received next term's teaching assignment. To your surprise, you find your teaching load includes a class in seventh grade Bible. Of course, you're a Christian, you're glad for this opportunity. You've read and studied the Bible—maybe in Sunday school, maybe in small groups, maybe even in college or Bible institute. But you've never had formal preparation for teaching the Bible in school. Where do you start? How do you teach the Bible to teenagers?

The place to start is by recognizing that the Bible is a book—granted a special book with special authority from a special source. But it is still a *book* made up of words, sentences, paragraphs or stanzas; it is marked off by commas, periods, question marks. In other words, the Bible is a collection of writings or literature—very special writings, to be sure, but literature nonetheless. As such, the Bible must be *read* to be comprehended; it cannot be absorbed through the skin or injected into the veins. It must be read using those same powers of intellect and reason with which we seek to read and understand any other literature.

Remarkably, the Bible can be read by anyone literate enough to read his hometown newspaper. But reading is far more than the act of passing our eyes over a page. It must also include the idea of ascertaining the facts through close examination; it must be a thoughtful reading, reading that animates letters of the alphabet, diphthongs, and syllables into words whose very sound is imbued with life and meaning. "One must be an inventor to read well," said Ralph Waldo Emerson. "There is then creative reading as well as creative writing." Emerson's observations apply as much to Bible reading as to any other.

To help us become better readers and students of the Bible, God gives to some Christians a particular gift, the gift of teaching. In fact, according to Paul, one of the signs that a man is qualified to be an overseer in the church is his ability to teach (1 Tim. 3:2). He also tells Timothy, "Until I come, devote yourself to the public reading of Scripture, to preaching and to teaching" (1 Tim. 4:13, NIV). Just how did Paul expect these three qualities—reading, preaching, teaching—to work together?

Teaching the Bible begins with reading the Bible. Of course, this Bible reading can be done privately and silently. But what Paul calls for—and what every good teacher knows is necessary—is public reading, reading aloud. This lifting up of Scripture from the eye to the ear is one of the most important ingredients of effective teaching, for it not only helps the substandard reader who may not have been able to make it through the text, or the lazy student who never bothered to try; but it also recreates the living experience of the text *at this very moment!* When Genesis 22 is read aloud in class or some other assembly, the whole drama is re-enacted in the theater of our minds. Once more the father and son climb alone to the top of the mountain. Once more the son asks his terrifying question, and the father gives his answer born out of implicit faith. Once again the son submits, and the father in his anguish obeys. Then comes the glorious voice of deliverance, the substitution of the ram, and the renaming of that place, "The Lord will provide." Left to silent reading—or worse, to an assumed reading that may never have taken place—the text languishes and lessons are lost. Read aloud, the Scriptures spring to life.

But they must be read effectively, and not everyone reads well in public. In twenty-five years of teaching English and Bible in secondary school, I have learned that every student needs practice and experience at reading, but not at the risk of ruining a good story or poem. I give my students plenty of opportunities to read aloud in class—their own essays, clippings from the sports pages, items from magazines. But when I want that class to feel Macbeth's horror at meeting Banquo's ghost, I do not entrust those lines to a faulty, stumbling, disabled reader. If necessary, I read the text myself or give the lines to carefully selected students who, I can be sure, will not mangle the text. The same is true in Bible classes. Sometimes to bring an important episode or scene to life, a group of faculty colleagues, all of whom read well, comes together and like a cast at a theatrical audition reads the text dramatically. But even these teachers, whose familiarity with the text may be taken for granted, meet to rehearse their reading, to receive instruction and direction in the kind of intonation and emphasis desired. Furthermore, as a lay reader of Scripture lessons in my local church, I am conscious of my obligation to lead the congregation into a fuller understanding of the particular passages from the Old and New Testaments. I read and rehearse my reading many times before taking my place in the sanctuary on a Sunday morning.

After reading, according to Paul, comes the dual responsibility of preaching and teaching. The word *preaching* brings to mind the pastor's Sunday sermon, but the Greek word Paul uses has meanings that go beyond the usual impressions of a minister's sermons as we generally understand them. Certainly there is a great need for us to hear and be challenged by the public proclamation of God's Word in a carefully organized and powerfully delivered speech. But we cannot confine our ideas of preaching to oratory; that does not seem to be what Paul is urging upon Timothy. Throughout the New Testament, where the word appears in several forms, preaching suggests a proclaiming (sometimes spoken, sometimes written) whose purpose may be to exhort or persuade or entreat or admonish; but always, to *encourage*.

In his Letter to the Romans, for instance, when Paul is enumerating the several gifts a Christian may possess, he writes,

> We have different gifts, according to the grace given to us. If a man's gift is prophesying, let him use it in proportion to his faith. If it is serving, let him serve; if it is teaching, let him teach; if it is *encouraging*, let him *encourage* (Rom. 12:6–8, NIV).

TEV agrees with NIV in translating the word "encourage." Other versions, KJV and RSV, use "exhort." Phillips calls it "the stimulating of the faith," while NEB says that "one who has the gift of stirring speech should use it to stir his hearers." Together these various translations give a fuller dimension to what it means to *preach*.

The public reading of the Bible together with encouragement or exhortation should always accompany our teaching of God's Word. As teachers, we give instruction in righteousness as we help students study the Scriptures and thus find guidelines for their lives. Reading the Bible carefully and thoughtfully should lead to the asking of questions to discover what it says and how it illuminates their path (Ps. 119:105).

PRINCIPLES FOR TEACHING

As you begin to prepare for a class in Bible, several basic principles will make your work easier and more effective.

1. Design your curriculum around Bible narratives. Teaching the Bible is an overwhelming task at best because of the Book's diversity and profundity. Effective planning by a department head, committee of teachers, or an individual teacher should take into account student ages and levels of experience and should then select appropriate passages of Scripture. Ideally, the material to be studied should progress in a developmental manner from the simple to the complex, from the childlike to the mature. For children and also for new believers, biblical narratives are essential to provide a basis for understanding who God is and how he has chosen to act among us. Concurrent with these biblical narratives, students learn doctrinal principles. As they mature in age and in spiritual growth, more complex teaching is suitable. But not until a foundation has been laid in Bible stories.

The gospel is the truth of God's creative and redeeming acts. This truth might have been expressed like an insurance policy, in language no layman can understand. It might have been written as a quadratic equation or an Einstein formula. It might have been uttered in the crescendos of earthquake, the tumult of wind, or the crackling of fire. But instead, like a still small voice, the truth we call Good News has been issued to us as *story*.

Not everyone at every age can reason through Paul's complex argument in his Letter to the Romans; not everyone can follow the development of the speaker's thought in Ecclesiastes, from bitterness to resolution. But everybody at every age loves a story. That's why a close reading and study of Bible stories must be the starting point in a Bible study curriculum. Among these should be the lives of Abraham, Isaac, Jacob, and Joseph; the adventures of Joshua, Gideon, Samson, and Esther; and the Gospel accounts of Jesus' ministry. For whenever these stories are dramatized in the imagination—when a teacher brings the words to life, giving flesh and blood to the participants in a story, when those characters take center stage in the theater of the mind—then, as Paul assures us (see 1 Cor. 10:6), what happened to the men and women in Bible stories serves as a lesson to us.

The value of the biblical narrative as a study project should never be underestimated. Paul focused on the importance of knowing the Bible when he wrote to the Romans, "For everything that was written in the past was written to teach us, so that through endurance and the encouragement of the Scriptures we might have hope" (Rom. 15:4, NIV). Much later he applied this truth to Timothy who had known the Scriptures from infancy and had thereby been made "wise for salvation through faith in Christ Jesus" (2 Tim. 3:15, NIV). Ultimately, the Gospel is "the old, old story/Of Jesus and His love."

2. Don't assume your students know the Bible very well. My observation as father, teacher, and churchman tells me that children today know considerably less about the biblical narratives than my generation knew. In our home, I believe my wife and I worked our way faithfully through various illustrated books of Bible stories; we had some recordings of dramatizations which we played till the grooves wore out. But today's boys and girls, even from homes whose name is a household word among evangelicals, are sometimes as ignorant as Tom Sawyer, who identified two of the twelve apostles as David and Goliath. In the church we seem to have made a compensatory swing from old-fashioned biblical instruction that ignored practical social issues to teaching that stresses personal application to daily life, but at the expense of factual Bible knowledge.

Much of that teaching, I submit, results from a faulty assumption, that a base for personal application can be laid upon cursory Bible knowledge. The fact is that, in general, Bible stories aren't being taught anymore in Christian homes; so the church and school must work to take up the slack.

As an added factor, we must also consider the problems caused by the fact that the Bible is a book and that some students and even adults don't read well, just as others don't manage elementary arithmetic well enough to keep their checkbooks in balance. As shown earlier, reading is a skill to be learned and practiced. Make no mistake: A substantial portion of every adult group fails to grasp primary meaning at first reading. Federally sponsored summer institutes for English teachers have made that fact distressingly apparent. Dull to the nuances of language, some people never get the point of a joke or the thrust of a Bible story. As Jesus himself said, it takes ears to hear.

3. **Use a variety of teaching methods,** such as:

- brief lecture followed by discussion;
- provocative questions;
- dramatization or role playing;
- dramatic reading.

The teacher who lectures all the time has chosen a closed-circuit method of communication, restricted to one-way speaker/listener engagement. A lecture may be a useful, even necessary, means of conveying blocks of information to a large assembly at one time; but any real teaching in connection with that lecture occurs only if, in spite of the size of the audience, the speaker is able to convince an individual listener that they two are communicating together. Even then, the lecturer and his listener lack the benefits of dialogue with its parry and riposte. Unless lecturing is followed up by close study of the text in small groups, where questions and answers flow freely, lecturing is an exercise in oratory.

Furthermore, the lecturer who never lays it on the line with his students, submitting to their questions, loses out on his own learning possibilities. For every teacher the most rewarding learning experience comes in that moment when a student surprises us with a new insight, when the current of class discussion spills over the banks of what we knew and floods us with latent knowledge. The fact is that, in every class, some students may raise questions better suited to learning than any I have invented. I must be open to this probability.

When a teacher's method of instruction lends itself to such openness, students are encouraged to speak up and, from their own experience with the text or their own sense of its application to their lives, express its meaning. But to make this happen, a teacher must remain flexible—not gullible and weak about being led down blind alleys, but willing to explore a fresh idea and see where it leads.

4. Integrate your Bible lesson with common experience. The great need in Bible teaching is to make its truth relevant to people today. As teachers, however, it isn't enough for us to talk about how up-to-date the Bible is; we must show its contemporaneity. We must deal with passages that speak to issues familiar in current events, contemporary art, or popular culture. If the Bible is God's articulation of his will and truth for his people, then the principles of that truth need to be made applicable to our lives. We can't afford to avoid troublesome matters or disagreeable topics and then expect Christians to have a proper foundation of biblical principles upon which to stand.

What are these issues? Homosexuality, abortion, euthanasia, biological experimentation, *triage* (the decision to let the weakest die to save the strongest), state control of personal and private liberties, ecumenicity, unification of world governments, disarmament, militarism, patriotism, theories of knowledge, marriage and divorce, equality between male and female, relationships between parents and children—these are only a few of the topics of vital concern today about which the Bible has something to say, whether explicitly or in principle. Will our students know the Bible's position on these matters? Only if we open up its pages to them and ask the Spirit of God to lead us into a knowledge of his truth.

Here, then, as an overview are the responsibilities of the classroom Bible teacher:

1. to read and clarify the text's meaning;
2. to encourage and exhort students to believe its truth;
3. to teach students to live by the Bible's principles.

But how can we best fulfill these responsibilities? What method of teaching should we follow? I suggest from experience that we learn to *ask questions,* using what is sometimes called "the inquiry method" or "inductive study" and letting the Bible answer for itself.

CHAPTER 2

The Question and Answer Method

There are many approaches to teaching the Bible. A linguist masters the Hebrew and Greek languages and works from the vantage point of his knowledge of the text's original languages. An anthropologist or historian brings what he knows of cultures and the events of history and then looks in the Bible for evidence of social development or cause-effect relationships in human events. Theologians construct their systematic outlines of dogma and their articles of faith based on what they find in the Bible. These all can be—and very often are—effective means of studying the Bible, but they demand prior qualifications of scholarship which few ordinary readers of the Bible possess. In fact, sometimes scholarship seems to become almost an end in itself, neglecting to remember that the Bible may indeed by understood on many levels by its "ordinary readers."

This is no cheap shot at scholarship—at learning classical languages or cultural anthropology or dogmatic theology. It is a reminder, however, that the Bible is a *book*, an anthology of writings, a library of literature; in short, a collection of narratives, poems, sermons, proverbs and other wise sayings, letters, lists of names, treatises, arguments, love songs, historical records, predictions and dire warnings, adventure stories, and so on. All of these appear as words-on-paper, arranged into a variety of literary forms intended to be read by anyone acquainted with the language into which the original Hebrew and Greek texts have been translated. So then, the starting point in studying and teaching the Bible is making sure that your own skills in reading and comprehending your own language are sufficient to read and understand the Bible.

PHASES IN THE QUESTION AND ANSWER METHOD

One of the best methods for teaching the Bible is by question and answer. By this method, both teacher and students together read the text open before them and examine it by asking questions, starting at an elementary level and developing an increasingly comprehensive scope to these questions. Each question leads to a variety of responses intended to teach, first, what the text says; then, what it means; finally, how its truth-principles apply to readers today.

Think of these three phases of Bible study as a staircase:

```
                              ┌─────────────────────────
                              │  HOW DOES IT APPLY?
              ┌───────────────┘
              │  WHAT DOES IT MEAN?
┌─────────────┘
│ WHAT DOES IT SAY?
```

The first level requires the use of reading skills for word recognition and grammatical relationships among words that form statements as sentences. By taking what we know of the English language and its conventions in writing, by using dictionaries to assist us in defining unfamiliar words, and by using the logic of sentence progression as these words appear on the page before us, we can achieve the first step, answering the question, "What does it say?"

The second step requires us to go beyond minimal reading skills of word recognition and sentence structure. At this next level we must look for meaning beyond the words themselves and even "between the lines." Meaning involves a complex interweaving of ideas, context, intention, form, mood, and effect upon the reader. It's rarely a simple matter to ask, "What does it mean?" or "What basic truth-principles are given here?"

It stands to reason that we must proceed up this staircase one step at a time. No one can begin to make application of the Scripture's teaching until, first, he or she understands what it says and what it means. Even then, the question, "How does it apply?" needs to be asked in two respects: personally and generally. For instance, how does the Bible's truth-principle of love for one's neighbor apply to me as an individual? Only after I've answered this question can I concern myself with applying the teaching to others and to the church-at-large.

An example of "Bible study" through the method of asking questions can be found in Romans 4. As Paul writes about the relationship of righteousness and faith, he refers his readers to the Book of Genesis (what we would call chapter 15) and asks them, "What does the Scripture say?" (Rom. 4:3, NIV). Later he asks them to consider when the event took place (Rom. 4:10) and throughout the remainder of the chapter considers the implications of Genesis 15 and the applications for later believers. Throughout the entire Epistle to the Romans, Paul uses questions to focus on specific points, to aid the readers' understanding, and to show relationships between one section and another. In similar ways we can approach God's Word with questions so that we may better understand its contents, meaning, and significance for our lives.

PREMISES OF THE QUESTION AND ANSWER METHOD

The premises on which this method of teaching operates are these:

1. The Bible is God's Word given as literature to be read and studied, using all the skills applicable to the reading of any written communication.

2. Study by question and answer can be done by anyone regardless of his prior knowledge of the Bible. As a student comes to a passage, he should not focus on what he already knows but should ask himself, "What does this particular section *say?* What does it *mean?* How does it *apply* to me?"

3. Study by question and answer limits its objectives to modest and manageable dimensions. Bible study of this kind grows in comprehensiveness, but it does not presume to skip all over the Bible at once. Instead it proceeds in small steps, examining in detail every verse of a chapter or paragraph, to the extent that the teacher's time and planning allows. A sound teaching principle recognizes that, if a student is taught to read one chapter of a novel or the first act of a play intelligently—that is, carefully taught how to ask the kinds of questions that can find their own answers in the text itself—that student can go on to read the rest of the text on his own, often without benefit of a teacher's presence. Therefore, a teacher should determine which chapters, paragraphs, verses may best develop the reader's own skills.

4. Studying the Bible by the question and answer method is not necessarily doctrinal study. It concentrates on a single passage, not a specific topic or doctrine. In time, as a student becomes familiar with the Bible in larger measure, he will be able to link up passages that speak together on some doctrinal matter. In every case, careful study of the Bible by question and answer should reveal the truth of that doctrine. But that truth must originate in the Scriptures, not in some volume of systematic theology.

5. Studying the Bible by this method is not necessarily evangelism. Because the written Word of God has power to convict its readers of their responsibility to God and need for redemption through the atonement offered by Jesus Christ, life-changing events result from studying the Bible. But Bible teaching, especially in a classroom setting, differs from other kinds of proclamation. The call to Christian commitment that comes from study of the Bible isn't motivated by eloquence or persuasive appeal or the dynamics of a mass meeting. Bible study is essentially a quiet, intelligent, introspective activity whose main purpose is communication with God through what he says in his Word. In this way Bible study acquaints every reader at close range with what the Bible itself—not some evangelist—says. Of course, we pray for the influence of our teaching to affect students' decisions. But the main thrust of our teaching is to provide a reasonable basis for those individual decisions to believe or not believe—decisions founded upon knowledge of what the Bible claims about God and his Son Jesus Christ.

6. Bible study by the question and answer method includes both *analysis* and *synthesis*. When I take my automobile to a mechanic for an engine overhaul, he takes the engine apart and asks—as it were—how each part is functioning. By asking questions about each part of a text, we are analyzing the text, breaking it down into smaller bits for easier understanding and assimilation. But almost anybody with a wrench can break apart an engine; it takes great patience and skill to put the parts back together again so that the automobile runs smoothly. In the same way, analysis needs synthesis, the act of putting back together into a whole the passage under scrutiny. Synthesis requires a responsive spirit in tune with the Spirit of God, ready to act out the truth-principles revealed through analysis.

But no doubt someone will say, "Why ask questions at all when the Bible is so clear about what it says?" Well, on the one hand, that appears to be a reasonable remark; on the other, it begs the question because the Bible can be far from clear on a particular issue. Witness the vast array of denominational and doctrinal divisions created among Christians, all of whom disagree and all of whom claim to know precisely why they are right and everyone else is wrong! The real point, however, is that questions addressed to the text help the reader to understand what it says and means and how it applies.

Of course, it would be possible to present the contents of the Bible in such a way that no questions were permitted or assumed to be necessary. Some alleged Bible instruction is given in just this manner. I recently heard a television Bible teacher declare that "the silver trumpets in the Old Testament speak of redemption." But he gave no further explanation; he gave no room for his audience to ask, "How so?" or "Why?" or "In what sense do musical instruments of a particular metal represent an action of God's grace?"

Many disappointed students of the Bible have had similar experiences with one teacher or another. Humility is the greatest asset a teacher can bring to his pupils—a realization communicated to his students that this teacher is also a willing learner. None of us has all the answers, particularly to our own difficult questions. Voltaire pointed out that a man must be ignorant when "he answers every question that is put to him." At the same time, by knowing how to ask questions we are helped to find their answers.

Bible study by this method of asking questions is no idle pastime. We study and teach the Bible in order to be able to run the great race and finish our course, having kept faith with the one who is to be our Judge. We are not merely indulging ourselves in shared ignorance, exchanging meaningless speculations about the Bible's teaching. There are answers to be found to our questions, and we ask those questions in a prayerful spirit, confident that, as Jesus Christ promised, the Holy Spirit will guide us "into all truth" (John 16:13).

CHAPTER 3

Jesus, the Master Teacher

As those beginning to teach by the question and answer method, we should be encouraged by several historical precedents. The apostle Paul has already been referred to in the previous chapter. Here we will briefly consider Socrates and then turn to the example provided by our Lord Jesus Christ.

One of great teachers of all time was Socrates, who lived in Athens from 470 to 399 B.C. His list of pupils and their students-in-turn includes Plato, who taught Aristotle, who taught Alexander the Great. Socrates' reputation in the fifth century B.C. as the wisest man in the world was based upon his own claim that among all men he was the most aware of his own ignorance, thereby making him the wisest! His method of teaching others depended on asking them questions, hoping by this means to open his students' minds by driving them to a deeper consideration of the issues. Often Socrates' questions assumed ignorance on his part, a device that has come to be known as "Socratic irony." But always the point of asking a question was to show how much more of a subject remains to be learned.

Jesus of Nazareth was the greatest of all teachers. As the Incarnate Lord of the universe, by whose word the world had been called into being (see Hebrews 1:1–3), he possessed divine wisdom. Yet as a teacher—a rabbi—he too followed the ancient practice of framing his lesson with questions posed to anyone who presented himself as a seeker-after-truth. Consider, for example, the setting of the parable of the Good Samaritan in Luke 10:25–37. It begins and concludes with questions. After the lawyer's initiating question, "Teacher, what must I do to inherit eternal life?" Jesus replies, "What is written in the Law?" Why does Jesus ask this question? Has he suffered a sudden lapse of memory? Why does he ask for information he already knows? Because Jesus is looking for a way to bring the lawyer face to face with more than a surface knowledge of the Law: Not the Law's content but its interpretation and application to the inquirer's life is what matters. So Jesus goes on to ask, "How do you read it?" When the parable has been told, Jesus again asks a question: "Which of these three do you think was a neighbor to the man who fell into the hands of robbers?" Once more, Jesus' purpose in asking the question isn't to obtain general information but to learn specifically how well his listener has grasped the meaning of his parable. The key words in Jesus' question are these: "Which . . . *do you think* . . . ?"

In numerous instances Jesus' first words to those he was about to heal or to those whom he would teach were in the form of a question. Choosing only a few pages from Luke's narrative, we can find these examples. To the rich young ruler Jesus replied, "Why do you call me good?" (Luke 18:19, NIV). To the blind man outside of Jericho he said, "What do you want me to do for you?" (Luke 18:41, NIV), as if it weren't perfectly obvious! When teaching from Psalm 110, Jesus asked, "How is it that they say the Christ is the Son of David? . . . David calls him 'Lord.' How then can he be his son?" (Luke 20:41–44, NIV). In Gethsemane he asked his disciples, "Why are you sleeping?" (Luke 22:46, NIV), and to Judas he said, "Judas, are you betraying the Son of Man with a kiss?" (Luke 22:48, NIV). On the road to Emmaus he asked Cleopas and his companion, "What are you discussing together as you walk along?" (Luke 24:17, NIV). Questions, questions.

There's a skill to asking questions, especially if we intend by our questioning to lead students to think more clearly about their reading and comprehension of the Bible. Some questions are more effective than others in uncovering the meanings of a text or at dislodging a reader's doubts or in bringing home a personal application of the text to the reader. We can see these skills illustrated in the example of Jesus' questions.

JESUS' USE OF QUESTIONS

First, Jesus always addressed his question directly to his audience. Whether in response to a previous remark or question—as when the rich young ruler asked how to obtain eternal life—or in general teaching, Jesus left no doubt as to whom he was addressing. In the great discourse in the temple (see John 10), when his enemies were about to stone him, Jesus faced them down with an ironic question:

> "I have shown you many great miracles from the Father. For which of these do you stone me?"
> "We are not stoning you for any of these," replied the Jews, "but for blasphemy, because you, a mere man, claim to be God."
> Jesus answered them, "Is it not written in your Law, 'I have said you are gods'? If he called them 'gods,' to whom the word of God came—and the Scripture cannot be broken—what about the one whom the Father set apart as his very own and sent into the world? Why then do you accuse me of blasphemy because I said, 'I am God's Son'?" (John 10:32–36, NIV).

We ought to frame our questions so that they address the specific audience before us—ourselves and our students—rather than the world-at-large. Our questions ought to generate personal involvement in our students; they should know that if they don't answer the question, it will go unanswered because there's nobody else to respond!

Notice, second, that Jesus' questions were always directed to the basic issue-at-hand. In John 10 his questions pointed to the unbelief of the Jews who did not really want to know who he was even though they asked, "How long will you keep us in suspense? If you are the Christ, tell us plainly" (John 10:24, NIV). Of course, the Lord Jesus Christ knew what prompted men to ask their questions "for he knew what was in a man" (John 2:25, NIV).

Jesus also knew the answers to the questions of those who were his disciples or his enemies, of those who were merely curious, or of those who really wanted to understand his teaching. Obviously, we lack his infallibility, his omniscience; nonetheless, we can follow his example. Like him, we should not evade any question, resorting to asking another question to avoid having to admit, "I don't know the answer to your question." This device fools no one, particularly our students, who readily recognize it and attribute it to our fear of losing respect. A perfectly acceptable response to any question beyond our capability to answer is this: "I don't know the answer to that question, but let's look through the Bible together and see if we can find an answer."

Furthermore, Jesus' questions grew out of an immediate situation and applied to that situation with unerring relevance. When someone in the crowd demanded, "Teacher, tell my brother to divide the inheritance with me," Jesus refused to engage in a legal dispute over the rights of brothers to their father's estate. Instead, he went right to the heart of the matter: the sin of greed. He asked, "Man, who appointed me a judge or an arbiter between you?" Then he went on to say, "Watch out! Be on your guard against all kinds of greed; a man's life does not consist in the abundance of his possessions" (Luke 12:13–15, NIV). His parable of the rich but foolish farmer follows in verses 16–21.

Jesus' questions were always brief and to the point. Long rambling questions lack directness. Asking an indirect question is like lowering a bucket into a well of water on a swinging rope. The looser the rope, the more the bucket swings and the harder it is to bring back a full pail of water. As a principle, we need to keep our questions short and pointed. Like Jesus, we need to avoid indulging ourselves in oratory when we mean to ask questions and elicit responses. Like the apostle Philip, who met the royal treasurer of Ethiopia, our question can be as direct as this: "Do you understand what you are reading?" (Acts 8:30, NIV).

Jesus' questions were always aimed at evoking some kind of response from his audience—an action that would affirm belief or confirm disbelief. Whether the subject was a point of Mosaic Law or a social convention, the questions Jesus put to his audience were intended to stir his listeners to make a commitment in faith. Sometimes, however, we may infer that his question bit so deeply that no answer was forthcoming; or perhaps the only answer was by a gesture or by a change in countenance, as when the rich young ruler responded to his exchange with Jesus by becoming "very sad" (Luke 18:23). On these occasions silence was its own answer; but at other times Jesus deliberately provoked his audience with his questions in order to force the issue, to draw a line between those who believed his gospel and those who chose not to believe. For instance, after the triumphal entry and the cleansing of the temple, Jesus was confronted by his enemies in the religious hierarchy.

> "Tell us by what authority you are doing these things," they said. "Who gave you this authority?"
> He replied, "I will also ask you a question. Tell me, John's baptism—was it from heaven, or from men?"
> They discussed it among themselves and said, "If we say, 'From heaven,' he will ask, 'Why didn't you believe him?' But if we say, 'From men,' all the people will stone us, because they are persuaded that John was a prophet."
> So they answered, "We don't know where it was from."
> Jesus said, "Neither will I tell you by what authority I am doing these things" (Luke 20:2-8, NIV).

After this head-on collision, it was only a matter of time until the religious leaders would express their disbelief with cries of "Crucify him!"

But there were also times when Jesus used questions to call forth declarations of belief. Notably, his questions at Caesarea Philippi illustrate his method. As we have noted, Jesus had no need to ask, "Who do people say the Son of Man is?" (Matt. 16:13, NIV); he already knew the opinions of the crowd. He asked that question not only to provide a contrasting setting in which to ask his disciples, "But what about you? Who do you say I am?" (Matt. 16:15, NIV), but also to give Peter and the others an opportunity to speak aloud for the first time what they had been whispering among themselves. Here was their chance to declare boldly that Jesus of Nazareth is indeed "the Christ, the Son of the living God" (Matt. 16:16). Again, following the Bread of Life discourse, when so many disciples had turned away from him, Jesus asked, "You do not want to leave too, do you?" Peter answered for the Twelve, "Lord, to whom shall we go? You have the words of eternal life. We believe and know that you are the Holy One of God" (John 6:67-69, NIV). In both instances Jesus had used a teacher's questions to draw out of his followers forthright declarations of faith. But he used such leading questions sparingly and always at points of crucial decision making, when his teaching had brought his audience to a crossroads where decisions to believe or not believe could no longer be waived.

JESUS' AUTHORITATIVE TEACHING

Some Bible teachers oppose the question and answer method on grounds that, since Jesus "taught as one who had authority" (Matt. 7:29, NIV), so must they. Yet it is perfectly obvious from the Scriptures themselves that such opposition to question and answers stems from a misreading of the Bible. We have already provided ample proof that Jesus' method of teaching depended to a large degree on asking questions and evoking answers. Yes, he was also didactic at times—lecturing, preaching, telling stories—but over and over again he returned to the simple inquiry technique. Even in the Sermon on the Mount, perhaps his most didactic teaching—and the passage preceding this observation about his authoritative manner of teaching —Jesus intersperses his declarations with numerous questions:

> . . . if the salt loses its saltiness, how can it be made salty again?

> If you love those who love you, what reward will you get? Are not even the tax collectors doing that? And if you greet only your brothers, what are you doing more than others? Do not even pagans do that?

> Is not life more important than food, and the body more important than clothes? Look at the birds of the air; they do not sow or reap or store away in barns, and yet your heavenly Father feeds them. Are you not much more valuable than they? Who of you by worrying can add a single hour to his life? And why do you worry about clothes? . . . If that is how God clothes the grass of the field, . . . will he not much more clothe you, O you of little faith?

> Why do you look at the speck of sawdust in your brother's eye and pay no attention to the plank in your own eye?

> Which of you, if his son asks for bread, will give him a stone? Or if he asks for a fish, will give him a snake?

> Do people pick grapes from thornbushes, or figs from thistles? (Matt. 5–7, NIV).

No, Jesus' authoritative teaching did not at all restrict him from asking questions. His authority did not derive from flaunting his omniscience but from the parallel between what he said and how he lived. When the temple guards came back empty-handed, having failed to arrest him, they gave as their excuse this character reference: "No one ever spoke the way this man does" (John 7:46, NIV). Were they commenting on his oratorical skills or his circus barker's persuasiveness? Certainly not. The guards had found an intensity in Jesus' manner of delivering his message and had seen in his face—as well as in the faces of his followers—an authenticity that was its own authority. And so, we must dismiss as inaccurate the supposition that to ask questions is contrary to Jesus' own method of teaching.

To be effective teachers of the Bible by the question and answer method, we need to follow these principles exemplified by Jesus:

1. Address our questions directly to our audience and to specific persons in our audience.
2. Direct our questions to the text and to any issues it raises.
3. Ask questions relevant to the text being studied.
4. Make our questions brief and to the point.
5. Aim our questions at evoking a response from our audience.

But we must always remember that in one major aspect of our teaching we must differ from Jesus' manner. He knew all the answers to his questions; we do not. Because he is the Incarnate Word, Eternal Wisdom, the Alpha and the Omega, nothing is beyond his knowledge. His questions, therefore, presuppose that omniscience. The purpose of Jesus' questions to his audience was not to acquire knowledge but to show his audience the path to truth. With us, it must be different. None of us knows all there is to be known about any subject, least of all the Bible; so we approach even the most familiar text with an expectation of learning something fresh and new to us. Furthermore, because we believe that the Holy Spirit has the power to quicken our minds, we must always remain open to the possibility of further teaching from "the Spirit of truth" (John 16:13).

We can never afford the luxury of arrogance in teaching the Bible. We need to bear in mind the wisdom of the Reverend John Robinson, the Pilgrims' pastor who, in his farewell sermon to those about to sail to the New World on the *Mayflower*, said these words: "I am very confident the Lord hath more truth and light yet to break forth out of his holy Word."

CHAPTER 4

What Does It Say?

For Christians words have special significance. First, we believe in a God who both speaks and writes, whose Word is to be heard and read, then obeyed. Second, we believe in a God in whose image we are created; thus our uniqueness as the only created beings possessing the divine attribute of verbal language. Third, we believe that when our God chose to make himself known to the human race as one of us, it was as the Word-made-flesh. So to Christians words are reminders of the Eternal Word, the Divine Logos, the Creating Word who is still "sustaining all things by his powerful word" (Heb. 1:3, NIV).

Words are signposts to ideas and narrators of action, pointing out our thoughts and telling us the details of our lives. From our earliest gurgle and babble as infants to our halting lisp as toddlers and on to our growth as mature adults, we attempt by means of language to express our thoughts and emotions; at the same time, we hope to acquire the capacity to listen to the speech of others or to read what they have written and thereby experience their thinking and feeling.

In order for us to share our language with others, we must share a common vocabulary, a reasonably common pronunciation, and in writing, a few commonly understood mechanics such as spelling and punctuation. When we travel from one region of North America to another, we often become startlingly aware of how different speech and usage can be. Mark Twain's story, "Buck Fanshaw's Funeral," illustrates the problem. When Buck Fanshaw dies, his best friend in the mining town of Virginia City goes to a newly arrived Eastern preacher, asking him to perform the funeral service. Some of the conversation between Scotty Briggs and the preacher goes like this:

> "Are you the duck that runs the gospel-mill next door?"
> "Am I the—pardon me, I believe I do not understand.... I am the shepherd in charge of the flock whose fold is next door."

"The which?"

"The spiritual adviser of the little company of believers whose sanctuary adjoins these premises."

Scotty scratched his head, reflected a moment, and then said: "You ruther hold over me, pard. I reckon I can't call that hand. Ante and pass the buck."

"How? I beg pardon. What did I understand you to say?"

Of course, the whole point is that neither Scotty Briggs the gambler nor the preacher understands one word of what the other is saying. The only way they can begin to communicate, however, is by asking questions of each other.

The same is true for us as students and teachers of the Bible. To begin to know what God's Word teaches, we must first know what its words say. Current language Bibles will make reading comprehension more easily achieved. Those who use Bibles translated in an earlier century should make sure that they are aware of the grammatical practices and vocabulary of whatever century is the source of their translation.

This pattern of study through inquiry calls for close attention to the words as they appear *on the page*—their specific arrangement into grammatical units as phrases or clauses, sentences making statements or asking questions; their special arrangement or *rhetoric* for purposes of effective description, explanation, argument, or details of storytelling. Because we assume that the Scriptures were written by careful writers with serious intention, we also assume that these words and phrases have been put together by choice, not by accident. God makes no slip of the tongue; his Word is truth, and so every reader needs to pay attention to what the Bible actually says. Only after a reader comprehends at the basic level can the next step toward *meaning* be successfully attained.

But what questions should be asked? Rudyard Kipling wrote,

> I keep six honest serving-men
> (They taught me all I knew):
> Their names are What and Why and When
> and How and Where and Who.

Suppose we are beginning to read John's Gospel. Asking the primary question, "What does it *say?*" really means asking supplementary questions such as these:

WHAT is the relationship between the Word and God?
WHY does the writer begin his narrative about Jesus with
    this discussion of the Word?
WHEN was the Word with God?
HOW are the Word and God related?
WHERE was this relationship carried on?
WHO is the writer talking about?

Or perhaps Paul's Letter to Philemon is the text to be studied. If
so, these are the kinds of questions we might ask to discover
what the words say:

WHAT relationship does the writer choose to adopt with
    Philemon? On WHAT basis?
WHY does the writer call himself "a prisoner of Christ
    Jesus"? Isn't it the Romans who have put him in jail?
WHEN does Paul expect to see Philemon again?
HOW does Paul persuade Philemon to accept Onesimus?
WHERE did Paul meet up with the runaway slave?
WHO else is in prison with Paul? WHO is not with him
    there?

DENOTATION AND CONNOTATION

Each of these questions consistently points us back to the
words-on-paper. To answer them we must be aware of the *denotation* or specific dictionary meaning of the words. For this
part of the Bible study, keeping some reference books close at
hand will be very useful. An English dictionary and a good
Bible dictionary provide help for words not in everyday usage.
For example, 1 Samuel 17:5,6 tells us that Goliath had armor
weighing five thousand shekels and that he wore bronze greaves.
Most of us will need to look up these words to discover what
kind of armor Goliath wore. Maps and atlases can also give us a
geographical orientation for distances between locations and for
the terrain of the countryside. See the list of Helpful Books at
the end of this volume for suggestions.

Of course, many words possess numerous denotations; until
such words are seen in their context, their meanings are ambiguous, subject to uncertainty. Take the word *fast; Webster's*

New Collegiate Dictionary shows four different parts of speech—as adjective, adverb, verb, and noun—and more than two dozen meanings in just one of those uses as an adjective! To describe someone as a "fast friend" might mean any of several possibilities:

1. a friend who is reliable;
2. a friend who runs quickly;
3. a friend with a reputation for wild behavior.

Ambiguity is a characteristic of language and its flexibility. It allows for a reasonable degree of uncertainty caused by a word's multiple meanings. Although we may claim to know what *fast* means, we cannot be certain of which of its several possible meanings applies best until we read the whole passage.

Beyond the ambiguity of multiple denotations, words also possess *connotations,* layers of added meanings that begin with the writer's perception of the word he uses and extend to the vast possibilities of every individual reader's reception of that same word. Words acquire meanings as they are used by different writers and readers in different cultures at different periods of history.

Most words have both *objective* and *subjective* meanings. Objectively, the word denotes what makes most sense in its given context; subjectively, the word connotes special meaning or meanings, first to the one who writes or speaks it, then to each of those who read or hear the word, depending on the experience of the audience. Consider the word *mile.* To anyone familiar with English measurement, this word denotes a standard distance of 1760 yards, 5280 feet, or 63,360 inches. But the same word connotes an abundantly rich range of responses from people according to their interests. Athletes and weekend joggers will summon up recollections of time and fatigue in running the mile. Shoppers may think of shopping centers named the "Miracle Mile"; residents of Denver may relate the word to altitude and their "mile-high city." Automobile dealers or mechanics will think of odometer readings and miles-per-gallon. Readers of poetry may recall the final lines of Robert Frost's "Stopping by Woods on a Snowy Evening":

The woods are lovely, dark and deep.
But I have promises to keep,
And miles to go before I sleep,
And miles to go before I sleep.

The possibilities for connotative meanings are endless. Thus we need to be alert observers of the words we read.

KINDS OF LANGUAGE

As we continue to analyze the words of the text, we must also ask, "What kind of language is addressing me here? Is it *figurative* or *literal*? If figurative, how can I best respond to it and find its meaning?" To illustrate, literal language intends to be taken at face value: If a writer says that a professional basketball player is 7'3", we know that this height is a *literal* fact; it can be measured and recorded. If the same writer says, "What a skyscraper that center is!" we don't go looking for a man who resembles the Empire State Building. We accept the writer's use of *figurative* language—a hyperbole making the comparison between a tall man and a tall building.

Stories or narratives use both literal and figurative language: literal language to give us details of time and place, the various participants in the action, what they're doing and why; figurative language to help us recognize an unfamiliar experience by a familiar—such as loneliness: "I feel as though I'd lost my last friend." The speaker (or *narrator*) hasn't literally lost his last friend, but he expresses the same kind of feeling. Or, "I was floating on a cloud" to express a lightness of spirit, a sense of being free from cares that would weigh down and make floating impossible.

Poetry, however, relies on figurative language far more than literal in that it makes use of the senses—sight, sound, taste, touch, smell—and the emotions—love, hate, joy, sorrow, security, fear. In Psalm 91:4, for instance, when the poet writes about God, "He will cover you with his feathers, and under his wings you will find refuge," the poet doesn't mean that God is a big bird or a mother hen. The poet simply uses a metaphor to suggest a comparison between the protection provided by a bird for its young, who hide themselves under the outstretched

wings of the parent, and the security provided by God. Referring to God as a protector reassures the speaker's fear.

Poetry relies upon figurative language to stimulate the reader's senses or emotions. Sometimes the meaning is immediately
apparent, as when God commands Moses to remind the people
of Israel "how I carried you on eagles' wings" (Exod. 19:4, NIV).
The comparison between the swiftness and security of the
strongest bird and God's care for his people hardly needs any
pondering. On other occasions, however, the figure of speech
requires a reader to pause and consider some of its subsurface
implications. In Psalm 1 the speaker uses a simile to describe a
man:

> He is like a tree planted by streams of water,
>   which yields its fruit in season
>   and whose leaf does not wither (Ps. 1:3, NIV).

Obviously the speaker doesn't expect us to see a human being
turned into an apple tree. But the speaker does expect us to
think about the qualities of a flourishing tree that might resem-
ble the characteristics of a happy and productive man or woman
of God. Here precisely is where the question and answer
method works so well. We can ask ourselves, "What are the
similarities between a mature believer and a healthy tree fed by
its roots in the riverbank?"

In this same psalm the speaker wishes to describe the man
who is literally happy or blessed by God. In the speaker's understanding of things, such a person must avoid intimate involvement with the enemies of God. But the speaker does not
come right out and baldly or literally say, "You will be happy
only if you have nothing to do with sinners and avoid any as-
sociation with God's enemies." Instead, as we know, the
speaker employs a series of verbal pictures to describe a man
who first walks, then stands, and finally sits down with God's
enemies. This figurative language takes on fuller meaning when
we see it like a motion picture of a person walking by a group of
people, stopping to converse with them, then accepting their
invitation to be seated and share their hospitality.

As we approach any passage of Scripture, we should make
sure that we know what it says and what kind of language is
being used—WHO is saying WHAT to WHOM; WHEN and

WHERE it is being said; WHY and HOW this event or emotion is developing. To help us understand what the words say, we may need to use reference tools such as dictionaries, atlases, or encyclopedias. We must be alert to the denotations and connotations of particular words as well as to distinctions between literal and figurative language. In Psalm 91:4 the answer to "WHO is a source of refuge?" is God, not a bird. Further insight into the passage can be gained as we move from "What does it *say?*" to "What does it *mean?*"

CHAPTER 5

What Does It Mean?

Making known the meaning of language is the purpose of communication in language, just as conveying the meaning of gestures—shaking hands, waving a fist, applauding by clapping our hands—is the purpose of those gestures. Words exist to be understood. So the words of the Bible are given to be understood. But finding the meaning of any statement—in the Bible or anywhere else—may be somewhat more challenging than it appears on the surface. Why? Because the essence of meaning exists not only in what appears to have been said but also in the very manner and setting, the very shape and form of the passage, giving additional dimension to the meanings those words convey.

LITERARY FORMS

To discover meaning we must first see the passage of literature in its distinctive form—as a poem, a story, a parable, a prophetic warning, a genealogy, a general letter, or whatever. We must ask how the particular form of literature contributes to the effectiveness of the written message.

Poems and Psalms. We must look at poems or psalms as songs and ask ourselves what appears to be the reason for singing. Many recent translations help readers to notice the poetry of the Bible by typesetting poetic sections in a customary poetic format. Long sections of the prophetic books follow Hebrew poetic style and many readers appreciate a printed format which reflects this fact.

A wise teacher of poetry, Laurence Perrine, writes in *Sound and Sense:*

> The meaning of a poem is the experience it expresses—nothing less. But the reader who, baffled by a particular poem, asks

perplexedly, "What does it *mean?*" is usually after something more specific than this. He wants something that he can grasp entirely with his mind. We may therefore find it useful to make a distinction between the TOTAL MEANING of a poem—that which it communicates (and which can be communicated in no other way)—and its PROSE MEANING—the ingredient that can be separated out in the form of prose paraphrase (p. 148).

What Professor Perrine is telling us is of utmost importance to Christians, who believe in the mystery of words and the Word. He is saying that a poem *is* what it *is;* it cannot be itself and mean what it means in any other form than it expresses as a poem. No prose restatement of its ideas or emotions is the same as the poem. "The person I love is as beautiful and sweet as a summer flower" is not the same as these lines by Robert Burns:

> O my luve is like a red, red rose
> That's newly sprung in June.

To comprehend the "total meaning" of this poem and the loving sentiments it expresses, one must come to know the poem itself.

So too with Scripture. We may take the beautiful thoughts derived from a passage in the Bible, such as these words of Moses,

> The eternal God is your refuge
>   and underneath are the everlasting arms (Deut. 33:27, NIV),

and paraphrase them to read something like this:

> God is your hiding place and he supports you;

or this:

> The God who always was and always shall be is the same God
> who provides you with his never-ending care.

But these are poor substitutes. Both paraphrases are restatements of something resembling the ideas expressed in the biblical quotation—ideas of dependability, safety from danger, timelessness, loving support, physical and spiritual security. Why, then, are they so unsatisfactory? Why do they fall so short of expressing what the original—even in a modern English translation like the NIV—conveys? Perhaps because any paraphrase lacks the very power of incantation, the spell-binding effect of language, which gives poetry its grandeur and which common prose can never recapture. In short, no matter how skillfully we read or how creatively we restate the themes of a text, we must always remember that the fullest expression of what that text means is to be found in itself.

Story or Narrative. We must look at a story or narrative and ask why this story is being told and what it shows us about those to whom the story belongs—the participants in the action, the storyteller himself, his audience. We might even ask how a particular passage would have differed if, for example, a song had been written as a story, and vice versa. Exodus 14 and 15 give us an illustration in point. How does the song in Exodus 15 differ from the story in the preceding chapter? What does one passage have that the other lacks? How, then, do they complement each other? Narrative will be treated more fully in a later section.

Parable. A specific type of narrative or story is the parable, a brief anecdote with details paralleling a particular situation, usually told to make a specific point or to illustrate a religious principle. Questions on parables could include the following:

> WHAT occasioned the telling of the parable?
> WHO is the audience?
> WHAT is the main point?
> WHAT response is given?

Prophetic Warning. Prophetic warnings or predictions are often interspersed with historical narrative so that we must be careful to discern what kind of language is used. We should begin by noticing such aspects of grammar as verb tenses and conditions. Does the text say, "God *will* do something" or "The Assyrians *will* come upon you" or "*Unless* you do this," or "*Whenever* you do that"? Many prophetic sections are introduced by words such as "The word of the Lord came unto _____ saying...," "Woe," or "In that day."

Genealogies. Genealogical lists are often avoided in Bible studies, but if the student has a little background knowledge, they too can reward investigation. Pronunciation difficulties can be overcome by guidelines given in Bible dictionaries or

encyclopedias or even the *New Columbia Encyclopedia*. Genealogies can be seen as useful summaries of key persons and
their relationships. Taken all together they demonstrate the
people through whom God brought the Messiah into the world.
But even individual sections can give added light to historical
narrative; for example, 1 Chronicles 2:15,16 demonstrates that
Joab was David's nephew, a useful fact to keep in mind when
reading the accounts of David's life. First Chronicles 11:41 lists
Uriah the Hittite as one of David's mighty men who "gave his
kingship strong support to extend it over the whole land" (1
Chron. 11:10, NIV). This gives an extra dimension to the story of
David and Bathsheba. As you read genealogies and other lists of
names, ask yourself:

WHY is this section given?
WHERE do these people fit in the historical narratives?
HOW are they related to each other?

Letters or Epistles. We should look at letters or epistles with
their particular format in mind: Usually both the addressee and
the writer are given near the beginning of the letter (as was the
custom in ancient times) together with some phrases of com-
mendation. The body of the letter presents the main topics,
often divided into a section giving the doctrinal basis and
another giving the practical application of the subject(s). The
final verses may include personal greetings, benedictions, and
doxologies.
    Relevant questions about letters might be:

WHO is the writer? TO WHOM is he writing?
WHERE are they located?
WHAT is the writer's attitude toward the audience?
WHAT main ideas are emphasized?
WHAT problems are mentioned?
WHY is the letter being written?
WHAT kind of background of the readers is presumed?
    (For example, are there any Old Testament quotations?)

CONTEXT

Meaning comes first from form, then from context; in other words, we must look at various passages or whole books of the Bible as literature-in-context. Elements of context include historical and geographical setting, social customs, cultural arrangements, theological development, and other factors surrounding a given event or piece of literature. Biblical history took place thousands of years ago in Near Eastern countries which had a culture that differed from ours in many respects. Human nature does not change, but its manifestations can; and as God revealed more of himself throughout the Old and New Testament, he expected people to respond to his continuing revelation.

We must keep these historical and social factors in mind as we particularly focus on the literary setting of a Bible passage which is itself a smaller part of a story, poem, letter, or other form discussed earlier. We cannot extrapolate meaning from a word or phrase by taking it out of its original setting and giving it a slanted reading to suit our own wishes. We have to take into account how a particular incident or episode fits into the whole narrative; how a specific argument fits into the whole letter; how a single statement fits into the context of a psalm or prophecy as a whole. When we have done this, then we are ready to discuss the question, "What does it mean?"

We do considerable damage to the meaning of Scripture whenever we misread the context of a passage. Consider, for instance, a familiar passage from Isaiah often cited by persons wishing to testify to "the leading of the Lord" in their lives. According to the KJV, Isaiah 30:21 reads, in part, "This is the way, walk ye in it," and this section is the most often quoted. Certainly it appears to speak about "the leading of the Lord." Here seems to be a clear declaration of direction and the command to obey its signposts. But what do we find when the text is read in its complete setting?

A careful reading of this portion of Isaiah's prophecy reveals that the prophet is spelling out the promise of God's redemption, in spite of Israel's waywardness. Through his prophet God rebukes Israel's penchant for straying:

"Woe to the obstinate children,"
  declares the Lord,
"to those who carry out plans that are not mine,
  forming an alliance, but not by my Spirit,
  heaping sin upon sin" (Isa. 30:1, NIV).

Israel's sin has been to ignore God's divine leadership, operating independently of God, "without consulting me" (Isa. 30:2, NIV). As proof of rejecting God's authority, Israel launches on a series of tangents away from God's will.

This is what the Sovereign Lord, the Holy One of Israel, says:
"In repentance and rest is your salvation,
  in quietness and trust is your strength,
  but you would have none of it.
You said, 'No, we will flee on horses.'
  Therefore you will flee!
You said, 'We will ride off on swift horses.'
  Therefore your pursuers will be swift!" (Isa. 30:15–16, NIV).

Even so, the Lord offers mercy and compassion in welcoming his wandering people back to the path marked out for them. This is the context in which the prophet then says,

Whether you turn to the right or to the left,
your ears will hear a voice behind you, saying,
"This is the way; walk in it" (Isa. 30:31, NIV).

Why is the voice coming from *behind?* Because God's headstrong people have run ahead and gone down the wrong fork in the road. Like silly sheep running ahead of the shepherd, God's people have arrogated leadership to themselves. So the voice they hear is not the *leading* of the Lord but the reasserting of his right to lead and of our lostness unless we follow.

The extended treatment of this point should serve to remind us of the importance of making sure that we have adequately considered the literary context of a verse as we study its meaning. Since chapter and verse divisions do not form part of the original text, we may sometimes need to remind ourselves that more than one chapter may be needed to cover a complete episode or an entire argument.

UNIFYING FACTORS

A procedure which will help us to define the extent of a passage
for study is to find the unifying factors of the story or poem—
what holds it together, giving the text coherence and structure.
When we see a building under construction, we see its foundation and framework, its girders and crossbeams; we may see
workmen driving nails or fastening rivets or applying mortar
between the bricks. A piece of writing, to stand on its own, also
needs to be held together by rivets—words expressing unifying
ideas. These may include such conjunctions as *therefore,
wherefore, thus, because, although, unless,* and *if,* and such
phrases as *as a result, at that time, in that day.*

Narrative Structure. In a story the unifying features are its
characters, plot, setting, and theme: WHO is doing WHAT,
WHERE, WHEN, and WHY. Somebody is involved in circumstances that bring him into conflict with other people; these circumstances occur at a certain specific time and place. Working
together, these components of the story or narrative give it
unity. Its structure may be built upon a series of developing
episodes that mark the story's beginning, middle, and end; or its
structure may appear in a recurring theme.

For example, look at the parables in Luke 15. Each of these
three teaching stories concerns the loss and subsequent finding
of something precious—a sheep, a dowry coin, a son. The entire
chapter is built upon a structure of climactic order, moving from
one event of significance to an even greater event: from *lost* to
found. But within the chapter there is also an element of
climactic order, from the sheep whose value is calculable, to the
coin representing all the woman's financial resources and security, and on to the son whose worth to his father is beyond estimate. Another element of structure is completeness. In the concluding story, Jesus begins by saying, "There was a man who
had two sons" (Luke 15:11, NIV); then he proceeds to tell about
the younger son. But to make the story complete, we know that
the storyteller must return to talk about the older son, or else he
would not have bothered mentioning both sons. Although often
ignored in sermons about "The Prodigal Son," the elder brother
completes the story and gives it unity.

Poetic Structure. In examining the structure of poetry in the Bible, we need to recall that much of its poetry is intended to be sung. The psalms are still sung today in some form in most churches—as congregational hymns such as "The King of Love My Shepherd Is," as choral anthems or solos, and as canticles in the liturgy. Young people have also been able to sing them in a folk style because of the special characteristics of Hebrew poetry. Whereas English poetry often depends for unity upon patterns of rhyme, rhythm, and meter, Hebrew poetry achieves structural unity through *parallelism* and *antithesis*.

Using parallelism, the poet makes a statement, then restates the same idea in a second line, re-emphasizing the original statement:

> I will extol the Lord at all times;
>   his praise will always be on my lips (Ps. 34:1, NIV).

> All day long I have been plagued;
>   I have been punished every morning (Ps. 73:14, NIV).

In antithesis, the writer makes a statement, then shows its opposite line of thought in the second statement:

> The lions may grow weak and hungry,
>   but those who seek the Lord lack no good thing (Ps. 34:10, NIV).

> Plans fail for lack of counsel,
>   but with many advisers they succeed (Prov. 15:22, NIV).

The importance of parallelism and antithesis rather than rhyme as a feature of Hebrew poetry has made it possible to translate using the parallel *ideas* rather than rhyming *words*. A reader should observe the addition or emphasis made by the parallel lines of poetry; if one could read every other line to get the basic idea, what do the parallel sentiments contribute?

Another structural pattern in the poetry of the Bible is *cause and effect*, by which the poet describes a situation and then shows what the outcome will be. Sometimes the pattern is in two stages:

> Fear the Lord, you his saints,
>   for those who fear him lack nothing (Ps. 34:9, NIV).

Notice the threefold stages in the next example:

This poor man called, and the Lord heard him;
   he saved him out of all his troubles (Ps. 34:6, NIV).

Another unifying feature of biblical poetry comes from the
extended use of a figure of speech or *analogy* throughout the
poem or song. We shall see when we study Psalm 23 more
closely how the poet maintains an analogy between God the
Shepherd and himself as a sheep belonging to God's fold.
Another example may be found in Psalm 69:

Save me, O God,
   for the waters have come up to my neck.
I sink in the miry depths,
   where there is no foothold.
I have come into the deep waters;
   the floods engulf me.
I am worn out calling for help;
   my throat is parched.
My eyes fail,
   looking for my God (Ps. 69:1–3, NIV).

In the lines that follow immediately, the speaker explains that
his enemies are numerous, his shame great. We soon realize,
therefore, that the deep waters and fear of drowning are not literal but figurative. Yet they are no less real, for they represent
real dangers to him—dangers that would overwhelm him, dangers that would pull him under, dangers that might cause him to
lose his life and even his faith. He is drowning in shame and
being sucked under by his enemies. But the speaker still has
hope:

But I pray to you, O Lord,
   in the time of your favor;
in your great love, O God,
   answer me with your sure salvation.
Rescue me from the mire,
   do not let me sink;
deliver me from those who hate me,
   from the deep waters.
Do not let the floodwaters engulf me
   or the depths swallow me up
   or the pit close its mouth over me.
Answer me, O Lord, out of the goodness of your love;
   in your great mercy turn to me (Ps. 69:13–16, NIV).

This lengthy analogy of a drowning man's pleas for help

creates a dramatic effect upon the reader. We cannot skip over such a psalm without seeing and hearing and feeling the terror of a drowning man—someone caught in the quicksand of a tidal pond, for instance—and sharing that same fear. By expressing his predicament in such dramatically visual terms, the poet is also able to make his rescue dramatic and all the more joyous. When we read the psalm and transfer the poet's experience to our own, we may also be able to share his faith and his ultimate deliverance—not from physical drowning, but from sinful shame:

> I will praise God's name in song
> and glorify him with thanksgiving (Ps. 69:30, NIV).

VOICE

To discover meaning we must also look at the ways in which words are being used to create impressions in our minds. Early in our reading we must learn to ask, "Who is speaking to me in this text? What voice is addressing me?" Robert Frost once said, "Every poem is dramatic. Somebody is speaking to somebody else." The same can be said about any piece of writing. From the words-on-paper we obtain an impression, as it were, of a human voice speaking to us, a real human being addressing us, exhorting us, informing us, humiliating us, encouraging us, confessing to us, reminiscing with us—in short, *talking* as though we were face to face.

One of the first responsibilities of any reader is to make this metaphorical identification: to ask, "Who is speaking in this poem or story?" Remember, this is not a question of authorship; we aren't asking, "Who wrote this poem or story?" The question concerns *rhetoric:* By what purposeful arrangement of words and phrases does the writer project a "voice" speaking to his reader? What is the nature and character of that voice?

In Psalm 23, for example, the speaker declares himself to be one of the Lord's sheep; he characterizes himself by adopting the characteristics of that animal—needing care, needing food and water for sustenance, needing rest for refreshment, needing a safe path, needing protection, needing an occasional prodding of the Shepherd's crook to keep in line. The speaker isn't a sheep, but by using these metaphors we recognize in him the human equivalents to a sheep's needs.

We may also infer from the psalm that the speaker knows something about sheep: their habits, their needs, and the means a shepherd uses to care for and control them.

The author of this poem could have written, "The Lord is my King" or "The Lord is my Doctor" or "The Lord is my Teacher." But the author would then have needed to invent a different speaker to talk to us about the Lord as King, Doctor, or Teacher; the speaker-as-sheep wouldn't have been an appropriate choice, and thus the entire psalm would have been different:

> The Lord is my Teacher: I'm well instructed.
> He gives me the finest books to read;
> He discusses the most complex issues so that
> I can understand them.
> He knows when I need a break and sends me
> out for recreation and refreshment...

We should also consider the narrator's *point of view*. Is he a participant in the action or is he an observer of it? Does he have a special bias, or is he an impartial recorder?

Tone. Recognizing the speaker and his traits also allows us to recognize the tone with which he speaks—the attitude he manifests toward his audience (the reader) and toward his subject (the events he is narrating or the emotions he is expressing). In oral communication we listen to the sound of the speaker's voice and we watch gestures and facial expressions to discover his attitude. In written communication we must be alert to the choice of particular words and their arrangement to acquire the same kind of information. By analyzing how the speaker feels, we can certainly sense on whose side he stands, what opinion he holds, especially as it concerns God and his dealings with human beings. In most of the narratives, the speaker assumes that God is just and righteous and must not be opposed. In some of the psalms, however, the speaker argues with God, contests his will, concedes reluctantly to that will.

Humor. An important element of tone sometimes overlooked by readers of the Bible is its ironic humor. Incidents in Bible stories are often surprising, with unexpected twists and turns in the circumstances and in the telling of a story. For instance, in Genesis 40, Joseph interprets the dreams of two fellow prisoners, Pharaoh's chief cupbearer and chief baker, telling each that "within three days Pharaoh will lift up your head" (Gen. 40:13, NIV). When the prediction comes true, the text says,

> Now the third day was Pharaoh's birthday, and he gave a feast for all his officials. He lifted up the heads of the chief cupbearer and the chief baker in the presence of his officials: He restored the chief cupbearer to his position, so that he once again put the cup into Pharaoh's hand, but he hanged the chief baker, just as Joseph had said to them in his interpretation (Gen. 40:20–22, NIV).

Obviously, the shock of this chilling reversal of the chief baker's expectations brings both a shudder of fear and a grim chuckle at the irony of his doom.

Elton Trueblood has written an important study called *The Humor of Christ*, in which he shows how greatly Jesus' teaching relies upon a wry use of language, playing upon words and sometimes employing sarcasm. For instance, Trueblood refers to Jesus' use of "preposterous statements to get His point across" as in the lesson on how hard it is to enter the kingdom of God: "It is easier for a camel to go through the eye of a needle than for a rich man to enter the kingdom of God" (Mark 10:25, NIV). Trueblood comments:

> By making the statement in such an exaggerated form, termed by Chesterton the *giantesque*, Christ made sure that it was memorable, whereas a prosy, qualified statement would certainly have been forgotten. The device is mirrored in our conventional Texas story, which no one believes literally, but which everyone remembers (pp. 47–48).

But humor in the Bible may also be sarcastic: excoriating as in Jesus' condemnation of the Pharisees' self-righteousness, mocking as in Elijah's challenges to the priests of Baal on Mount Carmel, or even gentle as in Jesus' greeting to Judas Iscariot, "Friend, why have you come?" (Matt. 26:50, NIV). In each case we need to be responsive to the ways in which humor affects the tone of a Scripture text.

Recognizing the speaker—his character, his tone of voice— helps make our reading of the Bible a humanizing experience.

No longer is some faceless, anonymous, pious voice from outer space addressing us. We can see, hear, and identify with the messenger who brings the message; we can dramatize the action and the conflicts of which the text speaks. By using our imagination, we can hear the earnestness in the voice of Paul, see the frown on the face of King Agrippa, and listen to the sarcastic way in which he retorts to the prisoner's defense, "Do you think that in such a short time you can persuade me to be a Christian?" (Acts 26:28, NIV). We can make the Bible come alive in our minds. When it does, it's amazing how much more of its truth we understand.

To summarize, after we have the content of the passage clearly in mind, we must then ask what additional factors should be considered. We proceed to observe the text and to ask questions about these other literary characteristics: form, context, unifying factors or structure, and speaking voice or tone.

CHAPTER 6

How Can Its Truth-Principles Be Applied?

In his book *Exploring the Bible: A Study of Background and Principles*, Frank E. Gaebelein concludes with a chapter entitled "Some Laws of Bible Interpretation." The most important law is the "Law of Spiritual Discernment." Of this principle Gaebelein says,

> In his first Corinthian epistle, Paul states the Law of Spiritual Discernment with characteristic power. Emphasizing the point that the Christian revelation transcends human wisdom, the great apostle continues as follows: "Eye hath not seen, nor ear heard, neither have entered into the heart of man, the things which God hath prepared for them that love him. But God hath revealed them unto us by his Spirit: for the Spirit searcheth all things, yea, the deep things of God. For what man knoweth the things of a man, save the spirit of man which is in him? even so the things of God knoweth no man, but the Spirit.... But the natural man receiveth not the things of the Spirit of God; for they are foolishness unto him: neither can he know them, because they are spiritually discerned" [1 Corinthians 2:9–14, KJV] (pp. 178–79).

Gaebelein makes it clear that "spiritual discernment" does not eliminate the need for careful reading. He advocates reasonable, logical analysis of literary forms and context, with comparison of figures of speech throughout the Bible as a whole, and always with proper regard for the limitations which the Bible imposes upon itself. For instance, the Bible does not presume to be a comprehensive textbook on the history of all ancient peoples. The Bible focuses on the origins and destiny of the descendants of Abraham, Isaac, and Jacob. So "spiritual discernment" comes after the individual Christian reader has done his part, using the natural skills with which God has already endowed him. Then, according to Gaebelein, one thing more remains to be done: *Pray as we read and study.* "And as we pray," he writes, "understanding of the divine message will come. For it may be set down as axiomatic that true discernment in the interpretation of God's Word is in direct ratio to the prayerfulness of the interpreter."

After we have prayerfully investigated what a given portion of Scripture says and what the words mean, by asking the questions given in chapters 4 and 5, we will still need to give further attention to the questions, "How should the meaning of these words be interpreted?" and "How should these words be applied?" These serious questions of *interpretation* (hermeneutics) and *application* will deepen our understanding of God's Word.

INTERPRETATION

Biblical interpretation is as old as the Scriptures themselves. In the times of Nehemiah and Ezra the scribe, the Word of God had its interpreters. We read that, when the wall of Jerusalem had been completed, the people were gathered together, and Ezra read aloud the entire law of Moses. Then the Levites divided the crowd into groups and "instructed the people in the Law while the people were standing there. They read from the Book of the Law of God, making it clear and giving the meaning so that the people could understand what was being read" (Neh. 8:7–8, NIV).

Just as interpretation began early, so did the need for application: Moses' final instructions to the children of Israel pointed out the need for all the people to hear the law so that they could "follow carefully all the words of this law" (Deut. 31:12, NIV). Following God's instructions after they have been understood is an important part of Bible study.

Of course, problems caused by different views of how Scripture should be interpreted have also been with us for a long time. As centuries passed and there were no longer prophets speaking for God, not all interpreters of the law agreed, just as today various attorneys and courts disagree on interpretations of the United States Code. By the time Jesus began to teach, a great body of conflicting opinion had grown up. Several Jewish sects interpreted the written Word of God, the Torah and the Prophets, according to their own understanding. For instance, the Pharisees and Sadducees, corresponding to what we might call, respectively, liberal and conservative factions, differed greatly in their interpretation of Moses' edict regarding retribution for personal injury: "But if there is serious injury, you are to take life for life, eye for eye, tooth for tooth, hand for hand, foot for foot, burn for burn, wound for wound, bruise for bruise" (Exod. 21:23–25, NIV). Sadducees held literally to the law's demands, but Pharisees no longer interpreted the law to mean that an eye must be gouged out or a limb cut off to pay for injury to someone else. Instead they read and interpreted the law to mean that, while the offending party was liable to make restitution to the injured party, this restitution could be in the form of a sum of money to compensate for the loss of an eye, a hand, a foot, and so forth. As Jesus taught, he gave yet a different interpretation from either of these. He did not allow for restitution in flesh and blood or in money.

> "You have heard that it was said, 'Eye for eye, and tooth for tooth.' But I tell you, Do not resist an evil person. If someone strikes you on the right cheek, turn to him the other also" (Matt. 5:38–39, NIV).

The greatest verification of the need for biblical interpretation found in the Bible itself may be in the postresurrection story of Jesus and his two mourning disciples on the road to Emmaus. After questioning their reason for gloom and being told of their doubts about the Christ in whom they had come to believe, Jesus said to them,

> "How foolish you are, and how slow of heart to believe all that the prophets have spoken! Did not the Christ have to suffer these things and then enter his glory?" And beginning with Moses and all the Prophets, he explained to them what was said in all the Scriptures concerning himself (Luke 24:25–27, NIV).

What a Scripture lesson that must have been! After the Risen Lord had made himself known in the act of breaking bread with them, the two disciples said to each other, "Were not our hearts burning within us while he talked with us on the road and opened the Scriptures to us?" (Luke 24:32, NIV). This ought to be the effect of our teaching and interpreting the Bible: Our students and we together should begin to experience something of the transcendent power of the Risen Lord, the warmth of the illumining Spirit of God, as we study the Scriptures.

Consider one of the ways Jesus described those disciples: "slow of heart to believe." As we approach the Scriptures, we must approach them in faith, even though we often face the fact that God has chosen to communicate his message in ways designed to be a mystery. This means that we confront the mystery of the Incarnation, say, with faith-to-believe that God really and truly did reveal himself in human form as Jesus of Nazareth. It's this act of believing-through-faith that unlocks the mystery of God's message. We have no other key.

Noah is a good example. He did not know by experience what a flood might be, but he took God at his word, believing through faith that deliverance or salvation would come only through obedience. As the New Testament tells us, "By faith Noah, when warned about things not yet seen, in holy fear built an ark to save his family" (Heb. 11:7, NIV). The prophet Daniel's faith enabled him to interpret the Word of God given both in dreams and in the eerie handwriting on the wall. Neither of these two manifestations of the Word of God was self-evident. Those pagans to whom the messages came could not interpret them. It took the man of faith to tell what they meant. But to those who have no faith-to-believe, the Word of God remains inscrutable, unknowable. Thus the Word of God through Isaiah to disbelieving Israel is an ironic puzzle, challenging them to try to understand the message without believing!

> Go and tell this people:
>   "Be ever hearing, but never understanding;
>   be ever seeing, but never perceiving."
> Make the heart of this people calloused;
>   make their ears dull
>   and close their eyes.
> Otherwise they might see with their eyes,
>   hear with their ears,
>   understand with their hearts,
> and turn and be healed (Isa. 6:9–10, NIV).

Similarly, when Jesus taught in parables, many in his audience were left baffled and confused. His disciples asked why he chose to leave his lessons ambiguous and without a concluding interpretation. Jesus made it clear that his teachings were not intended to be available to all listeners but only to those who acknowledged him as Lord:

> "The knowledge of the secrets of the kingdom of heaven has been given to you, but not to them. Whoever has will be given more, and he will have in abundance. Whoever does not have, even what he has will be taken from him. This is why I speak to them in parables" (Matt. 13:11–13, NIV).

Then quoting from Isaiah the passage above, Jesus continued, "But blessed are your eyes because they see, and your ears because they hear" (Matt. 13:16, NIV). The disciples' faith entitled them to Jesus' own interpretation of his parable of the sower and the seed. He left no doubt as to what the parable means, no possibility of error in interpretation.

Not all of the Scripture has been interpreted for us. But because of God's concern in giving us a written revelation, the truth of Scripture is guarded from error by the Holy Spirit himself. God commissioned particular men, like Habakkuk, who heard this word of command:

> Write down the revelation
>   and make it plain on tablets
>   so that a herald may run with it (Hab. 2:2, NIV).

Is it possible that those men so chosen by God could write in error? Of course not. They were not speculating or reasoning in their own minds; they were not weighing the possibilities or inventing stories or predicting the future like carnival fortunetellers. The apostle Peter assures us,

> You must understand that no prophecy of Scripture came about by the prophet's own interpretation. For prophecy never had its origin in the will of man, but men spoke from God as they were carried along by the Holy Spirit (2 Peter 1:20–21, NIV).

Just as the writers of Scripture themselves were inspired by the Holy Spirit, so should we also pray for wisdom and expect to be "carried along by the Holy Spirit" as we read and study. Thoughtful reading, intelligent use of our faculties to understand and appreciate the nuances of language, consistent and reasonable comparison of passages—these qualities in a prayerful student will help bring us to a satisfying answer to the question, "What are the truth-principles in this passage?" When we pray for an understanding of God's Word, we cannot be led into error, because we have the promise from Jesus Christ himself that "when he, the Spirit of truth, comes, he will guide you into all truth" (John 16:13, NIV).

Prayer is essential to Bible study, but prayer must be accompanied by study that takes into account the whole teaching of Scripture. That study is best conducted as an experience shared with others. We need the blessing of private devotions, but we especially need the benefits of public study of the Bible, whether in formal school, college, or seminary settings, in church classes and meetings, or in neighborhood groups. Here we have the example of Paul, who taught at Ephesus daily for three years. He tells the elders of that church,

> Guard yourselves and all the flock of which the Holy Spirit has made you overseers. Be shepherds of the church of God, which he bought with his own blood. I know that after I leave, savage wolves will come in among you and will not spare the flock. Even from your own number men will arise and distort the truth in order to draw away disciples after them. So be on your guard! (Acts 20:28–31, NIV).

Paul is warning against insidious private interpretation contrary to the doctrines the apostles had been teaching. All cults and other "savage wolves" who pervert Christian doctrine are fueled by the premise that only their founders have a wisdom which enables them to interpret Scripture rightly. Always these private interpretations deny some or another of the historic doctrines taught in the Bible and set down by the earliest church councils—such as the Council of Nicaea in 325, at which the church declared that God the Father and God the Son are "of one substance"—or the great declarations of faith such as the Westminster Confession.

Cultists routinely disregard the authority of the church as "a witness and a keeper of Holy Writ," as the Church of England's *Thirty-Nine Articles* of 1571 proclaims. Instead cultists assert their individualism as a higher virtue, rejecting those beliefs commonly held throughout the church since its beginning. Is it any wonder, therefore, that people such as Mary Baker Eddy or

Joseph Smith or Charles Taze Russell, founder of Jehovah's Witnesses, or any of the other cult leaders have been able to find ways to interpret the Bible so that its alleged meaning suited their heresies? To avoid being duped or ignorantly led into error, we need both prayer and the shared experience of study with others who can help to check us from fallacious reading and teaching.

We must, of course, show discernment in our choice of those whom we allow to teach us. Nobody can claim to possess the secret revelation withheld from all the rest of us. When Paul told Timothy that, although himself was held in prison chains, "God's word is not chained" (2 Tim. 2:9, NIV), a rich metaphor was made available to us. At one level of meaning Paul was saying that the Word of God is free to be expressed and received wherever it will and that no magistrate, emperor, or other hostile force can lock it up and impede its message. But at another level Paul's statement also suggests that no one who reads and teaches the Scriptures has the Word of God under lock and key either. None of us so thoroughly comprehends the mystery of divine revelation in its written form that we have it in our hip pocket, exclusive of anyone else's understanding.

Many of the cults have found that claiming an exclusive understanding of the Bible is an excellent way to propagate their teachings. Some of them are quite zealous in the ways they spread their version of what the Bible says. When I came home the other day, I found a handwritten letter tucked in my front door. It was from a representative of a cult who introduced herself as "one of Jehovah's Christian Witnesses." The letter was very gracious, inviting our family to begin a Bible study group in our home. What interested me about the letter was the writer's assumptions about the book to be studied. "The Bible is a very confusing book to most people," she wrote, "and can only be understood by those whom God inspires with his Spirit." Then she offered to come to our home "for one hour a week to study and share with you what I have learned." In other words, this Jehovah's Witness missionary was saying, "You can't understand the Bible without our particular key to unlock its secrets."

Many sincere Bible readers have indeed fallen prey to the idea that some special secret is a necessary basis for understanding the Bible. As a result they have accepted misrepresentations of biblical teaching. Why is this so? How is it possible for intelligent young people to spend hour upon hour in so-called Bible study and come away from it all believing that the absurdities of Sun Myung Moon's Unification Church are founded upon sound biblical warrants? There are no pat answers to this question, but one element to be credited is the power of Satan to deceive.

The apostolic writers were fully conscious of the early church's vulnerability to deceivers. Over and over they warn their readers to be on the alert against troublemakers, schismatics, teachers of contrary doctrine—such as denying that Jesus of Nazareth had come in human flesh (see 2 John 7)—and other heresies. "By smooth talk and flattery," wrote Paul to the Romans, "they deceive the minds of naive people" (Rom. 16:18, NIV). Such deceivers, he told Timothy, are themselves deceived, believing the heresies they teach and thereby making themselves all the more dangerous (see 2 Timothy 3:12–13). The only way to avoid being deceived by misinterpretation of Scripture and Christian doctrine is to heed Paul's advice to Timothy:

> But as for you, continue in what you have learned and have become convinced of, because you know those from whom you learned it, and how from infancy you have known the holy Scriptures, which are able to make you wise for salvation through faith in Christ Jesus (2 Tim. 3:14–15, NIV).

Here is the strongest antidote against the poison of deceitful interpretation: Any teaching of Scripture that robs Jesus Christ of his Lordship is Satan-inspired, a repeat performance of the temptation in the wilderness. He is the Lord Jesus Christ, co-eternal with God the Father Almighty and with the Holy Spirit. This is what the church has believed since the apostles; this is what the church has affirmed in the words of its earliest baptismal creeds—"Jesus Christ is Lord"—and in its historic councils since A.D. 325.

To counteract these possibilities of wrongly handling the Scripture, we need to adopt sound principles of interpretation. *Eerdmans' Handbook to the Bible* offers four helpful questions to aid us in this task:

> What did the passage mean to its original readers?
> What is the main point or teaching of the passage?
> How does it compare with other, perhaps clearer, Bible passages?
> If it was written to meet particular needs at the time, what is the general principle? (p. 58).

These questions glow with common sense. There is nothing particularly sanctified about them; they are the same sort of reasonable questions a reader of any ancient document would do well to ask. And as for those difficult passages whose meaning seems so murky, we are well advised by St. Augustine, who wrote, "In those places where things are used openly we may learn how to interpret them when they appear in obscure places" *(On Christian Doctrine,* Book III, Chapter 26). How much foolishness will we avoid if our biblical interpretation follows these sensible principles!

Eerdmans' Handbook to the Bible is itself one of several useful tools which may help to provide answers to the questions about the original readers and their world. It includes photographs and discussions of people, places, and objects which may need to be taken into account. Other religious reference tools such as Alfred Edersheim's *The Life and Times of Jesus the Messiah* can throw light on customs referred to in the Gospels. Charles F. Pfeiffer has edited *The Biblical World: A Dictionary of Biblical Archaeology* which includes background acquired through archeological studies. Atlases such as *The Macmillan Bible Atlas* provide maps for most of the geographic locations of scriptural events. Also, general encyclopedias, ancient histories and biographies, as well as other ancient literature give us information about the original readers and the other people and events mentioned in Scripture. The needs and situation of those first recipients of the written Word may help us to understand how they would have interpreted a given passage.

Discovery of the main point of the whole passage must be based on answers to questions given in chapters 4 and 5 and on general reading skills. These skills include following the logic of an argument, seeing the way one episode relates to another, noticing repeated words, and discerning the attitudes of the characters or the speaker towards God.

Finding the relationship of one Scripture passage to others is in part a cumulative process. The more we study the Word, the more we can see its overall unity. As we read, we should constantly compare the current section with other parts we know, even as the Bereans did when they listened to Paul (Acts 17:11). Works such as *Nave's Topical Bible* and concordances can be useful aids to finding passages with words or ideas similar to those of the passage under consideration. Moving to these other verses *after* we have carefully studied the main text may help us to finish interpreting the meaning. New Testament quotations of or allusions to the Old Testament may also provide illumination.

Another kind of useful tool for comparing passages is the harmony, such as *A Harmony of the Books of Samuel, Kings, and Chronicles,* by William D. Crockett. Harmonies of the Gospels are also available. Set in parallel columns, similar passages from several books enable the reader to see what parts of an episode are given in which books and what details from one book may further help in the comprehension of another.

In discerning the truth-principles found in the passage, it is also helpful to compare several portions of Scripture. For example, the Lord may have commented on the situation, or Paul may have given a doctrinal interpretation of an Old Testament narrative. New Testament passages throw light on the general truths of the Old Testament that are meant for the contemporary reader's understanding.

APPLICATION

As we consider the truth-principles taught by a given passage of Scripture, we really are moving from interpretation to application. As we read the Bible, we are confronted by the demand that we live according to its principles. As the apostle James warns,

> Do not merely listen to the word, and so deceive yourselves. Do what it says. Anyone who listens to the word but does not do what it says is like a man who looks at his face in a mirror and, after looking at himself, goes away and immediately forgets what he looks like. But the man who looks intently into the perfect law that gives freedom, and continues to do this, not forgetting what he has heard, but doing it—he will be blessed in what he does (James 1:22–25, NIV).

If we profess to believe that the Bible is God's Word, we act upon that belief by obeying its commands and by following its principles. Even the incidents which were recorded in the Old Testament were written down as examples and warnings for us (1 Cor. 10:1–11; Ps. 78:1–8). After we understand a situation, we see how to act in that situation.

I was once part of a team of four teachers in an English class of twelfth grade boys. One of the poems we were reading and discussing with these teenagers seemed not to be of much interest to them. The poem was Ben Jonson's lament on the death of his seven-year-old boy, "On My First Son." Our students could not quite summon up the emotional equipment to handle the poem. As a team, we decided on this teaching device: Each of the four men would read the poem aloud and offer a brief explication of it, based on how the poem spoke to him personally, in order to try to show our students how important personal experience is in comprehending meaning. Each of us did his part—the first man, married but with no children; the second with only daughters, no namesake son; I was third, with sons one of whom is a namesake. But our fourth colleague could speak from experience paralleling that of the poet's. His firstborn son had died, and he could empathize with the poet's anguish and lead the class into a fuller understanding of what Ben Jonson meant when he said,

> Farewell, thou child of my right hand, and joy!

However, we need not be limited to sharing experiences with the writer. We can also take his words beyond his own experience, sometimes understanding more than the writer could have intended. For example, when David wrote in Psalm 139:9,

> If I rise on the wings of the dawn,
> if I settle on the far side of the sea,

he obviously knew nothing whatever about supersonic flights by the Concorde from Kennedy International Airport to London or Paris. He was stretching his imagination to its limits by suggesting how impossible it is to go beyond the presence of God; for he went on to say,

> even there your hand will guide me,
> your right hand will hold me fast (Ps. 139:10, NIV).

Now for those of us who have experienced air travel, the possibility of racing the sun and traversing several time zones—so that we arrive before we left—no longer astonishes us. Because of personal experience, we can find connotations in David's poetry that exceed what he intended.

But am I wrong to allow my mind to leap almost 3000 years from the time of David's psalm to the era of jet planes and space travel? Not if my application of the text grows out of a reasonable reading that does nothing to contradict the teaching of Scripture elsewhere. For the essential point in Psalm 139 has nothing to do with technology and travel through time and space; the real point, affirmed throughout the Bible, is that wherever I go and however I might get there, God is present. St. Augustine, writing around A.D. 400, argued that God in his omniscience prepared for just such variations in understanding. The Bishop of Hippo says,

> And certainly, the Spirit of God who worked through that author, undoubtedly foresaw that this meaning would occur to the reader or listener. Rather, He provided that it might occur to him, since that meaning is dependent upon truth. For what could God have more generously and abundantly provided in the divine writings than that the same words might be understood in various ways which other no less divine witnesses approve? (*On Christian Doctrine*, Book III, Chapter 27).

In one sense God's basic requirements for a holy and righteous life—given in the Ten Commandments and summarized by Jesus of Nazareth as love for God and love for neighbor—are like tourist signs. Presumably all of God's revelation of truth could have been expressed in terse commands. But for reasons of his own, God has chosen a different form of communication. Because Christians know the Second Person of the Trinity as the Word, we are able to glimpse a little of the mystery and divine origins of language. Just as God himself cannot be contained or reduced to a formula—not even when the Word becomes flesh—so the attribute he shares with us, in communicating through words, will also elude our attempts at mastering it. This is the very nature of language. Scholars discussing *Hamlet* or legal experts arguing over the Bill of Rights are all able to read the document before them; they are looking at the same words. But because language is dynamic rather than static, because words pulsate with life, their interpretation must also be dynamic and responsive to living realities.

In practice, the question and answer method is useful when considering the application of a passage to our lives. Here are some suggestions:

1. How do the principles found in this passage apply to my personal life? To my thoughts? To my activities? To my goals?
2. How do these principles affect my life as part of a family? As part of a congregation of believers? As a citizen in society?
3. How do these principles apply to our school? Our church? Our nation as a whole?
4. Are there specific commands to obey? Are there examples to follow or to avoid?
5. Does my cultural setting affect my responsibility? For example, there are no longer slaves either in Rome or America. How do we apply Paul's specific instructions to slaves and masters?

These questions can be used regardless of the form of Scripture under study. We have already been reminded that Old Testament *narratives* were designed as examples and warnings. King Josiah (2 Kings 22,23) heard the Book of the Law which had been lost for years. He followed its commandments and made many changes in Judah; nevertheless, the *prophecies* of punishment for disobedience (e.g., Deut. 31:29) were carried out on God's people, although Josiah himself did not live to see the disasters.

Some prophecies are given long before their fulfillment, but as we see the fulfillment of some of the shorter term prophecies, we can apply the principle of God's reliability to the others as well. Of course, we must be part of the general audience to whom a promise is given before we can apply it to ourselves. As we read *poetry* such as Mary's Magnificat (Luke 1:46–55), we can share in her rejoicing because of God's greatness and mercy even though none of us is in her situation.

The New Testament *epistles* were for the most part directed to specific congregations, and as we read these letters we are struck by the fact that our lives are very similar to theirs. Thus we have little trouble understanding how to apply these books to ourselves.

Regardless of the passage we approach, we can be assured that all Scripture is useful for "training in righteousness" so that we "may be thoroughly equipped for every good work" (2 Tim. 3:16,17, NIV).

In summary, the key to sound Bible interpretation is faith supported by prayer, which leads to spiritual discernment. Then must follow comparison of various related passages to discover what Paul called "the whole will of God" (Acts 20:27, NIV). As we do so, we'll also learn how a particular historical event or personal lesson can have general and specific application as a principle of God's truth.

In our response to the Bible's truth-principles, we should follow the instructions of J. A. Bengel, who wrote in 1734, "Apply your whole self to the text: apply the whole matter to yourself." When we allow the powerful Word of God to speak to our lives, we have no choice but to put into practice those truths we have read and heard.

PART TWO

Ten Sample Lessons
on the Life of David
and Selected Psalms
with Unit Test

LESSON 1

Background and Context; Psalm 8

Enough theory. It's now time to demonstrate how teaching the Bible by the question and answer method works. For a model, we'll assume that a class proposes to read and study the life of David—shepherd, poet, king—in the books of Samuel, First Kings, and First Chronicles, and in the Psalms.

For these lessons you will prepare, first, by carefully reading and re-reading and re-reading the Scripture texts, always praying for that spiritual discernment that is the Holy Spirit's gift. Then, you will also read sufficient background material to know something of the history, cultures, and geography of Palestine a thousand years before Christ.

Among the kinds of information which may be useful are population, climate, food, family structure, monarchies, types of buildings, transportation, and distances. A summary sheet or two which will serve as the basis for the introductory lesson can be prepared for the class to use as a study guide. Depending on the age and background of your students, you may wish to include information on the human authors of the biblical books. Since there is no claim within the text as to who wrote most of the narratives, you may wish to discuss the possible authors, the sources of their materials, and the dates of writing. The books of Samuel and Kings were part of a larger history including Joshua, Judges, and Ruth; First and Second Chronicles were written later. Because he is the link between Eli, Saul, and David and his heirs, Samuel, the prophet and judge, is the central figure in these turbulent years in Israel and Judah, around 1050 B.C.

Of course, your most important teaching tools will be, first, the Bible itself and, second, the carefully structured questions you will prepare to lead the group into a closer reading of the text.

To open the first lesson you might begin by reading together Psalm 8. Then ask the class what they can tell about David after reading this psalm. They may already know a great deal. If so, ask for information which can be a background framework for the study: for example, what is a rough date for David's life? (If you get 1000 B.C., you are doing well!) Who else in the Bible lived in that time period? Where did David live? Can a student find the country on a globe or world map? What were houses like? What kinds of transportation were used? How were the battles fought? What books in the Bible give information about David's life? Why is David an important character for Christians to study?

At this point you will probably wish to distribute your summary sheets and point out basic kinds of information which you have decided will be useful. You may have several reference books to recommend for student use. Spend some time with a map so that students will have some idea of the geographic relationships and distances involved. Ask the students to draw a rough map of Palestine on which they can indicate the specific locations of the important sites in David's life—Bethlehem, Jerusalem, Philistia, Hebron, the wilderness of Judah, and so on. You may rather choose to use the map prepared for this book, or locate others in Bible atlases.

Next, you will want to introduce David, reminding your class that David is important as a king to whom God made great promises, as the ancestor of Jesus Christ, as the writer of many psalms, and so forth. But at the time we first meet him, David is one of those ordinary people—a teenager who is too young to be considered eligible for the military draft, but old enough to care for his father's sheep; a teenager, like many today, who likes to spend his free time picking out his own tunes on a stringed instrument and writing his own words. But he is also somebody who has begun to know God and to trust him. Although he lives to be seventy, he never achieves perfection, but his experiences can help all of us to follow God.

You may also have time during this first period to give your class an introduction to the methods which will form the basis of the study. You may need to reassure newer Christians or those who know little about the Old Testament that this question method will allow them to participate fully in the class. A

Bible passage will be read aloud and will be followed, first of all, by questions of basic comprehension: What's going on in the story? Who is doing what? Where? When? Why? Supplemental questions (marked in italics) are also provided for use in developing fuller responses to primary questions: What *else* is going on? What are the inner reactions of the participants in the story? What are the consequences of the action? Suggested answers give only an indication of what you might expect from a reasonably well-motivated study group; an exceptional group of readers, of course, will go well beyond the limits of these suggestions. Room has been provided in the margin for questions you have developed. Also, as a reminder of the concepts discussed in chapters 4, 5, and 6, key literary terms are printed in the margin in the first few lessons and from time to time thereafter to help you see the relationship of the theory to these sample lessons.

Be careful to keep students in the text at hand until most possibilities have been exhausted. Some students like to stray away on a tangent so that they may miss the main point. Encourage students to make sure that they know what the passage says and means before they attempt to apply a particular truth-principle to their lives.

As you do move into the application section of the lesson, you can focus on the human beings who are much like those of us who live 3000 years later, even though we may not be shepherds or kings. Like them, we are accountable to God and we find ourselves with similar problems—such as, conflicts with the government, battles with others in our family, and sexual temptation—and with similar prospects—such as, serving God in our careers, praising God for his guidance and protection, and enjoying his goodness and mercy.

LESSON 2

1 Samuel 16; Psalm 23

BACKGROUND

The story of David begins with Samuel—the son born to Hannah because of her faith, dedicated to serve God from childhood; the boy-prophet to whom God confided his rejection of Eli because of Eli's failure as a father; the judge over God's people and the prophet of the Lord whose dwelling was the shrine at Shiloh.

In 1 Samuel 8, we read of Israel's insistence on having a king like the other nations. Eventually Saul is anointed king, and his reign begins auspiciously with victories over Israel's perennial enemies, the barbaric Philistines. With his son Jonathan to succeed him, Saul's dynasty seems secure. Then moral disaster strikes. Saul disobeys God's direct command, given through Samuel (1 Sam. 15), to destroy the Amalekites; instead, he shows himself weak and pliable, deferring to the greed of his people. For this sin God rejects Saul and his family. In a striking scene, the desperate Saul grabs at the cloak of Samuel as he is about to leave the king; the cloak tears in Saul's hand. Samuel turns to Saul and says, "The Lord has torn the kingdom of Israel from you today and has given it to one of your neighbors—to one better than you" (1 Sam. 15:28, NIV). Saul's wretchedness is complete.

This lesson's reading selection should be divided into three parts: 1 Samuel 16:1–13, 1 Samuel 16:14–23, and Psalm 23. You could take an entire teaching period for each part, or you could spend less time on each if your group has difficulty in responding to the questions.

1 SAMUEL 16:1–13: READ ALOUD

WHAT DOES IT SAY? WHAT DOES IT MEAN?

Character

1. As this chapter begins, how does Samuel feel?

Tone

What is God's attitude toward Samuel?

Although Samuel is a man of God, devoted to serving him, he loves Saul and laments the circumstances that have brought Saul into disgrace before the Lord. Samuel knows that Saul has been rejected and must therefore die and be replaced as king. It is possible to discern in the voice of the Lord just a faint tone of rebuke, as though he were telling Samuel, "What's done is done; stop moping about it and get on with your work."

2. What task does God give Samuel to perform?

How will this task enable Samuel to overcome his depression?

Samuel may be a friend of King Saul, but he is before everything else a prophet of the Lord God of Israel. As such, his primary concern is to be obedient to God and to care for the nation, as he had for many years as judge. If God has rejected one king, the best remedy for Samuel's injured spirit is to accept the will of God and begin the process of anointing a king to succeed Saul. The message from God is quite specific—or at least, specific enough until Samuel needs further instructions. Here we can see a truth-principle to apply to our lives: Doing what God tells us will help us overcome our own feelings of fear or inadequacy.

Truth-principle

3. Why does Samuel hesitate?

Why should he fear the consequences of the task God has given him?

Why would Saul take any notice of Samuel's anointing somebody else?

Character

How does Samuel's question reveal his understanding of Saul's character?

Samuel is a judge and prophet, but Samuel is also a man subject to the same fears as anyone else. Saul is a tall, strong man with all the power of the king; rejected now by God, what would he have to lose by killing God's prophet? Saul could probably remember his own anointing (see 1 Samuel 10:1–16) and its secrecy. Samuel hesitates because he is momentarily afraid, and for good cause, humanly speaking.

Plot

4. What is God's plan to enable Samuel to obey him without risking his life?

Interpretation

Is God telling Samuel to be dishonest?

God instructs Samuel to use an apparent purpose for his visit to Bethlehem in order to fulfill his real mission without angering Saul. It's perfectly normal for the prophet to offer a public ritual of sacrifice and invite worshipers to attend. He can look over his audience and select the proper time to anoint the Lord's new king. The plan is in the same spirit as Jesus' instruction to his disciples to be "wise as serpents and harmless as doves." Both the motive and the means to its end are honorable. (Saul's later actions against David show that prudence was a wise characteristic for Samuel to have.)

5. Why are the elders or leading men of Bethlehem alarmed at Samuel's arrival?

Tone

What does their question to Samuel really mean? What is their tone of voice?

What preparation for the sacrifice does Samuel order?

Motive

What is Samuel's purpose in holding the public rite of sacrifice?

Several reasons may suggest themselves. Samuel is—next to Saul himself—the most important man in the kingdom. Any time he arrives somewhere, presumably, his hosts want to be fully prepared to honor him. But on this occasion he arrives unannounced. This can only mean a matter of great urgency; yet the elders of Bethlehem know of no such urgency that would summon Samuel in this manner. Does he, therefore, know something they don't? Has he come to disclose some dreadful secret or prophecy to them? Has he come to judge them for some wrong? Samuel's condemnation of Saul is a public matter, and Saul's despair must also be well-known. With the leaders of the nation in a distressed state, the citizens everywhere will also be uneasy. So their question upon greeting Samuel is asked in nervous agitation. They are honored by his presence, but they would prefer not to see him under such questionable circumstances. "Why didn't you tell us you were coming?" they seem to be saying beneath their layers of civil protocol. To set them at ease, Samuel assures Bethlehem's elders that all is well and orders them to get ready for a sacrifice according to the Mosaic law. In so doing, Samuel is following God's instructions to gather the entire male population of Bethlehem, including the family of Jesse, without arousing suspicion or undue curiosity.

Cultural
Context

6. Why does Jesse the father introduce Eliab, then Abinadab, then Shammah to Samuel?

The father simply follows the conventional order of introducing his eldest son and presumed heir first; then the second son, and so on through the seven sons present. The custom isn't uncommon even today. When an entire family is presented to strangers, it's not unusual for parents to indicate the order of age by saying, "This is Tom, Dick, and Harry." Not to have introduced Eliab first, however, would have been a grave insult to the eldest son. The occasion of meeting a man of Samuel's stature doesn't occur more than once in life. To the eldest belong certain privileges and honors. For instance, Rachel may not be married before her older sister Leah (see Genesis 29:26); in the parable, the elder brother is insulted that the father spreads a banquet for the younger son before ever offering him the same honor (see Luke 15:29). So, if any privilege were to be forthcoming from Samuel upon his family, Jesse would naturally expect it to be bestowed upon Eliab.

7. What is Samuel's immediate reaction upon meeting Eliab?

Why is he impressed with Eliab's potential to be king?

Samuel thinks that he has found God's replacement for Saul in Eliab. Here is another tall, handsome man (see 1 Samuel 9:2). It's important to note that Samuel is counseled by God not to place his priorities in external appearances.

Truth-
principle

8. Why does God reject Eliab?

How does God evaluate character?

On the humorous level perhaps it can be said that God has had enough trouble with tall, handsome kings! God doesn't judge by appearances, the way most of us judge political candidates; God examines the heart. By this

Inference

statement we can infer that Eliab was better-looking than his character would reveal. This judgment is borne out in 1 Samuel 17, where we again meet Eliab under somewhat less favorable conditions and receive a true estimate of his character.

9. Why was David not present at the sacrifice?

Narrative
Detail

Why does the narrator bother to tell us about David's responsibilities as a shepherd?

As the youngest son, David has been given the chore of staying on the job while his older brothers receive the privilege of attending the sacrifice presided over by the prophet Samuel. It's important to the immediate details of the story to explain David's absence by reference to his sheepherding; it's also important to later elements of his story—his experience with wild animals which prepared

Theme

him for Goliath. Students with wide imagination may also be able to see the connection between David the shepherd-king and the Son of David, who is both King of kings and the Good Shepherd. It's also worth noting that, at the time of Jesus' birth, the shepherds of Bethlehem were especially selected to care for the flock of sheep from which came each day's sacrificial animal. Tradition held that from their watchtower (used to patrol and warn of robbers or predatory animals) the Messiah would first be seen. There is an unbroken historical connection, therefore, between the shepherd boy of Bethlehem and the Incarnation.

Narrative Climax

10. What is the climax of this story?

Samuel anoints David, and the Spirit of the Lord came on him. You may want to discuss

Symbol

the symbolism of oil in the Old and New Testaments to designate people "anointed" or chosen by God. In some churches even today the bishop or minister anoints with oil those who are being confirmed or ordained, or for whom prayer is especially being requested

Interpretation

(see James 5:14). Another aspect of this narrative is that in the Old Testament the Holy Spirit came on people for specific purposes, whereas in the New Testament Christians are commanded to live by the Spirit (Gal. 5:16; Rom. 8:9).

Interpretation

11. What do you suppose was the reaction of Jesse and his sons to Samuel's act of anointing David?

Application

> *How do we react when God does something we don't expect, perhaps even in our families? (How was God's choice of Jacob over Esau or his favor toward Joseph received by their families?)*

At one level, it's hard to imagine that the anointing wasn't taken very seriously indeed. After all, this was the prophet of God performing a highly sacred and symbolic act. The last time he had done it, a man became king. At the same time, nothing is ever recorded by Jesse, his other sons, or David himself about his anointing. In fact, David consistently refers to Saul as "the Lord's anointed" (see 1 Samuel 24:6–10). It's also important to notice that, as in the case of Saul's anointing, Samuel anoints David in private—not at the site of the sacrifice but apparently at home, in the presence of his family. Can it be possible that these brothers were so oblivious of their youngest brother's qualities, they never gave the anointing another thought?

After you have discussed these questions and any others brought up by your class, you can move ahead to the next episode, in which both David and Saul are seen.

1 SAMUEL 16:14–23: READ ALOUD

WHAT DOES IT SAY? WHAT DOES IT MEAN?

Character

1. According to verse 14, what causes Saul's spiritual and mental depression?

Interpretation

Why does God allow Saul to suffer this anguish?

Is there a relationship between Saul's disobedience and the Spirit's departure?

What cure do his servants recommend?

Application

Do you recognize any modern applications of their psychological theory?

The passage does not require us to assume that Saul became demon possessed. Saul knew that God had withdrawn his Spirit and blessing; into the vacuum of his life rushed a form of paranoia or persecution complex. Beginning with 1 Samuel 18, Saul's paranoia manifests itself in jealousy, suspicion, and outright homicidal mania. Apparently God allows Saul to suffer as the consequences of his sin. Although 1 Samuel 15:31 tells us that Saul worshiped the Lord after his disobedience, we do not read anywhere that he truly repented. Saul's servants, of course, have no way of curing his depression; they can offer only palliatives in the form of "mood music." Modern corporations often install sound systems playing soothing music by Muzak in their reception areas, lounges, elevators, and even on the assembly line. Muzak, by the way, advertises "psychological programming" through its musical selections. Some dairy farmers have experimented with playing music in their barns as a means of increasing milk production.

Character

2. How has David's reputation as a musician and courageous fighter been established?

Application

Which of my characteristic traits would be mentioned if someone were to describe me? David's musical ability, bravery, speaking ability, good looks, are all accompanied by the fact that "the Lord is with him."

This is one of several problem passages in the narratives of David. It's clear that David's reputation rests upon his accomplishments in the region of Bethlehem. Obviously his ability as a songwriter and singer has been recognized locally; so too his bravery in defending his sheep. One of Saul's servants, probably from Bethlehem, knows David's reputation. Saul needs soothing music, but the fact that a musician can be found who is also virile, red-blooded, and courageous makes David an appealing choice. We must bear in mind the

Episodic Style

process by which these narratives came together: Written years after the events, they tend to include all major episodes in a hero's life as oral history has recalled them. Sometimes, however, transitions between episodes aren't as smooth as we might demand of a modern writer.

Characters   3. What do you suppose was the reaction of
                 David's family to the king's request for
                 David to appear at court?

                 *Why does David's father prepare such a
                 lavish gift for the king?*

We have no record of his brothers' reaction.
Jesse, however, was apparently honored by
his son's recognition. He does everything
possible to make a good impression upon the
king, including sending a gift in token of
submission and loyalty.

4. What effect did David's music have upon
Saul's condition?

Apparently David was temporarily effective,
so much so that Saul loved him like a son and
requested that he remain in service at the
court. According to this passage, David also
became Saul's armorbearer.

PSALM 23: READ ALOUD

WHAT DOES IT SAY? WHAT DOES IT MEAN?

You might read from several versions for this, and the whole
class might enjoy singing it as well. The tune "Crimond" is
available in many hymnbooks. You might also make use of "The
New 23rd" by Ralph Carmichael.

Analogy   1. In calling God his Shepherd, what is the
                 speaker saying about God, himself, and
                 their relationship?

                 *What are some of the characteristics of
                 the Lord as Shepherd?*

Voice   *What are some of the characteristics of
                 the speaker as sheep?*

Students should be encouraged to discover in
the text and comment on such characteristics

as God's protective care and guidance, God's full provision, man's inadequacy and dependence. The use of this analogy may lead them to mention characteristics not specifically in the text: God's right as "owner" of the sheep; man's tendency, like sheep, to follow blindly.

2. What specific benefits does the speaker enjoy because he follows the Shepherd?

   How are the rod and staff used by a shepherd?

Rest, nourishment, refreshment or restoration, guidance, protection, and correction or discipline are all inherent in this text. Between the lines one might infer fellowship with other members of the Lord's flock as another benefit.

Kind of Language

3. How do we know that, in verse 5, the poet may perhaps change his figurative language so that he is no longer referring to God as a Shepherd or himself as a sheep?

   What personal reference to David's own experience can we find in verse 5?

Sheep don't usually eat at a table like human beings; they don't drink from a cup or chalice. The poet has suspended his analogy for the moment. God is now portrayed as the host at a sumptuous banquet where there is so much to eat and drink—so many blessings, perhaps—we can't contain them. It may be worth noting that, according to the code of honor in the Near East, anyone eating came under the protection of his host. An enemy would scarcely consider being so treacherous as to attack while that protection was available. The reference to anointing the head with oil has at least two meanings: the custom of offering scented towels and perfumes with

Cultural Context

which to cleanse and refresh the traveler before dining, and of course the sacred ritual of proclaiming God's choice of high priest or king.

On the other hand, some have seen in this verse a reference to the tablelands or mesas where grain was sometimes provided for the sheep. Water also was given in hollowed-out places and oil was used like medicine against parasites or against the heat of the sun. (See Philip Keller, *A Shepherd Looks at Psalm 23.* Grand Rapids: Zondervan, 1976.)

Word Meaning

4. Returning to the shepherd-sheep comparison in verse 6, why is it important to the speaker that "goodness and love" ("mercy," KJV) *follow* him?

Customarily the shepherd leads the sheep; sheep dogs friendly to the shepherd and the flock may be used to keep the sheep moving ahead, to force straying sheep back in line, and to warn of any animals of prey that might sneak up from behind and try to make off with a lagging sheep. One way of expressing this would be that sheep who follow the Lord are in turn followed by his promises of goodness and mercy, rather than by the evil and merciless wolves of Satan.

5. If the Lord is the Shepherd, what does the speaker mean when he talks about sheep dwelling in the Lord's house?

Cultural Context

Near Eastern custom called for houses in villages to be built with an area for some domestic animals to be kept inside an outer wall, not necessarily in the central living area of the family. Injured animals, animals about to give birth, highly valuable animals ("the fatted calf") might be kept in this special manner away from the rest of the flock or herd. The speaker seems to be saying that he enjoys the kind of relationship with God that is, figuratively speaking, very special indeed. He anticipates an unending relationship, throughout his life and forever.

Point of View

6. What evidence can we find in the poem that it was written by someone who knows sheep and the job of sheepherding from experience?

Students should be able to point to specific terms of reference or customs they now understand and realize that only a shepherd could write a poem with such authenticity.

7. Why might this have been an appropriate song for David to sing upon his arrival at Saul's court?

Students may speculate on a question like this. Perhaps David's recent experiences would cause him to sing about them. As yet he himself has no literal enemies at Saul's court; however, the spirit of depression or paranoia afflicting Saul is a kind of enemy, combating with David's music for control of Saul.

HOW DOES THIS APPLY TO ME?

1. Since we don't possess God's ability to see into someone else's heart, how are we supposed to evaluate a person's character? Differences between God's viewpoint and man's can also be seen in passages such as Matthew 5:21–48.
2. To what extent are we influenced by music and other forms of art and entertainment around us? How concerned should we be that this influence is healthy?
3. If God is the Shepherd, what ought to be the attitude of those who follow him through "the valley of the shadow of death"?

Add some questions of your own:

4.

5.

PUTTING THIS LESSON INTO ACTION

1. Draft a questionnaire asking people to respond to questions about the music they choose to listen to, the music they hear passively or involuntarily, and the effect this music has on them. Classmates may interview each other. In urban areas some students may wish to visit stores or office buildings where "background music" may be heard. Truck drivers or other frequent travelers may be asked how music influences them during travel. Invite students who do homework while listening to radio or recordings to experiment with silence. Students ought to *discover* rather than *predict* the results of this survey.

2. Have the class write a revised version of Psalm 23. Students who profess to be believers can change the analogy from shepherd and sheep to some other relationship. Students who do not profess to believe can be encouraged to identify some other leader they wish to follow.

3. Scripture memorization is always a worthwhile activity. During this unit of study, students should be encouraged— or even required—to memorize at least one psalm. Any student who does not know Psalm 23 may start with this famous poem.

LESSON 3

1 Samuel 17

BACKGROUND

This next episode takes all 58 verses of the chapter. Note the use of dialogue, which not only adds realism to the narrative, but also reveals character.

1 SAMUEL 17: READ ALOUD

WHAT DOES IT SAY? WHAT DOES IT MEAN?

Geographical Context

1. Why did the Philistines choose to attack Israel at this location?

Apparently the Philistine military strategy didn't call for a mass encounter, army against army. Their confidence was in Goliath and his intimidating strength. In a ravine Goliath could scarcely be ambushed by a large group of Saul's soldiers, and he could certainly handle any two or three men who might dare to attack him. For the purposes of their military plans, the location was suitable. Make sure you locate on a map the places mentioned.

Description

2. Describe Goliath's appearance. What does the narrator say about him? What does he say about himself?

Students will need to look in reference books to find estimates of weight and measure. Scholarship is divided over whether or not Goliath was actually over nine feet tall. Is the speaker possibly using hyperbole to describe a very tall man—as in 1 Samuel 9:2, where

Saul is described as being taller than anyone else by a head or more? Yet the details of Goliath's armor and weapons suggest accuracy rather than figurative description. His armor weighs some 125 pounds; his spearhead is comparable to the weight of two implements in track and field events, the shot and hammer: 16 pounds. Goliath boasts of being the Philistine champion and issues his challenge on a man-to-man basis.

Motive

3. What was Goliath's purpose in challenging the army of Israel day after day?

Tone

What is particularly insulting about his challenge?

Connotation

What is the significance of Goliath's word defy?

Dramatic Tension

What is the accumulated effect of his daily challenges for forty days?

Goliath hopes to intimidate Saul's army. As each day passes without a hero from Israel to accept the giant's challenge, fear among Saul's soldiers increases. One might almost say, the giant grows more gigantic! To increase his intimidating power, Goliath insults his enemies by calling them various rude names. The connotations within "servants" or "slaves" (verses 8–9) go beyond involuntary servitude; in barbaric societies slaves were also victims of sexual perversions. But Goliath's greatest insult is in his use of the word *defy*. He sets himself up in defiance not only of Israel and her troops but also of Israel's God (see verses 26, 36, and 45). By the time David arrives at the battlefront, Goliath's daily challenges have totally demoralized Saul's army. Building the dramatic tension is good preparation for the appearance of David.

Narrative
Principle

4. Why does the narrative introduce David and his family, in verses 12–15, as though we haven't met him before?

Throughout the narratives of Israel's history, a principle seems to be followed: Tell all that is relevant to a given episode and its heroes, even if this results in overlapping information. Writers of these chronicles adapted their information from oral storytellers. In making their selection and arranging their material, the writers show that they are more concerned with *meaning* than with some of the niceties of modern historiography. This story, for example, may have been a favorite in oral history; it may have been told quite apart from the rest of David's life story, in which case introducing his family would be important; and it may be recorded here precisely as it was repeated in oral history.

5. Why does Jesse send David to the battle-front?

Character

How does David's dependability give a good foundation for his future (Matt. 25:21)?

From verse 15 we can assume that David made regular trips to his brothers' encampment, probably to take them food and other supplies from home. Jesse is concerned, quite frankly, that his sons not be in any greater hardship than necessary. He may also hope to ingratiate himself and his sons with their commanding officer, perhaps to keep him from sending them into hazardous duty; so he offers the commanding officer a gift—or is it a bribe? You might wish to point out David's sense of responsibility (see verse 20). He doesn't abandon the one job he has just because another has been given to him; he finds someone to take his place.

Setting

6. Describe the circumstances at the time of David's arrival at Saul's camp.

What is the Israelite army's reaction to Goliath's challenge this time?

Character

What is David's reaction upon hearing Goliath's challenge?

What is the basis for David's reaction, in contrast to others around him?

Students should be able to construct an imaginative representation of the scene in the valley of Elah based upon their analysis so far. On this occasion, when Goliath shouts his defiance, the soldiers of Saul run away in cowardly fear. Not even the promise of a rich reward from the king can turn any of them to act courageously. David's reaction needs to be seen in light of verse 15: this isn't his first time visiting his brothers, and so it probably isn't his first time—in the last forty days—to hear Goliath and to see Israel's cowardice. David feels ashamed on behalf of the soldiers, the king, the nation, and the nation's God. His reaction stands in sharp contrast to the materialists around him, who can only calculate and decide that the reward offered isn't worth the risk. They never mention the name of God. David is the first to show the true nature of Goliath's blasphemy. Goliath is a pagan idolater; the Israelites are the army of the living God, who is not only their God, but is Jehovah Almighty whom all the earth should know.

Character

7. Why is Eliab so angry with David?

How does Eliab try to compensate for his embarrassment?

As the oldest of Jesse's sons, Eliab has been humiliated in the presence of his youngest brother. David has seen Eliab run away from danger; far worse, Eliab has overheard his upstart brother making noises like a potential volunteer. To cover over his own shame, Eliab bullies David. He offers no gratitude for the provisions David has brought; he accuses him, instead, of irresponsibility and disparages David's role as the keep of "those *few* sheep," as if the numbers mattered more than the care given. He further accuses David of being like the football fan who berates the losing team but wouldn't dare accept a uniform and get into the game himself. David, says Eliab, has come to watch the fighting— ironic inasmuch as there isn't any fighting going on because of Israel's cowardice. Students may be able to connect this insight into Eliab's character with God's reasons for rejecting Eliab as king.

8. How does Saul learn about David's decision to volunteer?

Description

> *How does David present his credentials to Saul?*

News travels fast, especially news of a voluntary act of heroism. David's question, Eliab's anger, the whole improbable circumstance of a noncombatant's willingness to accept the giant's challenge all come to Saul's attention. When Saul interrogates him, David describes his various experiences defending his sheep, attributing his skill and success to the Lord.

9. Why is David outraged against Goliath and his challenge?

> *What is the basis of David's assurance of success?*

Once again, Goliath's defiance is cause for

David's outrage. David's assurance rests in his trust in God. Past experience leads him to faith for the future. Put into the colloquial, David is willing to stack his God against the Philistine's pagan gods, with no doubt as to who will triumph.

10. Why does David decline to wear Saul's armor?

   What weapons does he choose instead?

If we remember that David has served as Saul's armorbearer (1 Sam. 16:21), then we know that David is familiar with Saul's personal weapons. But such weapons were made for the individual using them, and Saul is the tallest man in his tribe; obviously Saul's coat of mail and helmet aren't going to fit the smaller man. Furthermore, David isn't accustomed to fighting with a soldier's weapons. He is used to the outdoorsman's weapons—the sling and shepherd's staff. An important point here is David's refusal to be flattered into wearing the king's armor, which surely would have hampered him.

Conflict

11. Describe the contrasts between the two opponents as David and Goliath face each other.

   Why is Goliath insulted?

Cultural Context

   Why do the two champions exchange insults with each other?

Students should recognize contrasting size, age, experience, weapons, and expressions of confidence, among other details. Goliath is insulted because, after forty days, he at least hopes for a worthy opponent; instead Israel sends out a volunteer for whom the giant feels nothing but contempt. The insults he throws at David are countered by David's claim of victory. Such verbal thrust-and-parry is part of the tradition of heroic combat, present in Homer's *Iliad* and other major literature; furthermore, it goes on today at the weighing-in of two boxing champions prior to their fight. David is especially insulting when he threatens not only to kill Goliath but also to give his corpse to the scavenger birds and beasts. As we know from our own culture, leaving a body exposed without burial is a dreadful insult to the dead.

12. What secret weapon does David possess which Goliath can't understand?

    According to the narrator, what was to be the real significance of David's victory?

Goliath has his enormous bulk and terrifying weapons, while David appears to have only a shepherd's staff, a sling, and a bag full of stones. But David also has "the name of the Lord Almighty" in which he finds both protection and power. David isn't fighting for the honor of the family name, of Saul, or of Israel; David is interested only in upholding the name of the Lord, whom Goliath has defied. The real significance of David's victory is to be twofold: first, the whole world will recognize that the God of Israel is supreme; second, all who witness this fight will realize that "the battle is the Lord's," rather than belonging to the strength of men.

Narrative Development

13. Why does the narrator bother to tell us that David has killed wild animals (verses 34–36) when the main event is his killing of Goliath (verses 48–51)? What is the purpose?

In the first passage David tells Saul about his

exploits. His description is fairly vivid; yet we have only his word to go on. But in the second passage we are there as it happens. The narrator gives us a movie close-up with sound track—we are so close to David we can hear the sling whizzing over his head, we can hear Goliath's grunt of shock and pain, we can see the welt form on his forehead as the stone imbeds itself and stuns him, we can hear and see his awful collapse; then the cheers from Israel and the cries of horror from Philistia as David runs forward and hacks off the giant's head. The purpose in telling us about the killing of the wild animals is to give David credentials for volunteering to kill Goliath. If David hadn't killed Goliath, we wouldn't care whether or not he had killed the animals; now we're convinced he did.

Interpretation   14. Why does it seem that Saul doesn't know who David is?

This is a puzzle hard to solve. One reasonable suggestion is that Saul's mental and spiritual condition was sufficiently weakened by his loss of God's blessing—as well as the demoralization of his army's cowardice for forty days—that he was not in command of his memory. Another suggestion is that this incident in David's life may be out of chronological order, belonging perhaps before 1 Samuel 16:14–23, where David goes to Saul's court. This explanation, of course, would account for Saul's advisers telling him that David is a courageous man. Or again, Saul may be asking about the family, as it was the family who would be exempt from taxes and with whom arrangements for a marriage would be made. Or perhaps it may be that this important story was meant to be told out of the fuller context of David's entire biography, in which case it needs to be completed by Saul's question, "Who is he? Where does he come from?"

HOW DOES THIS APPLY TO ME?

1. How does David's experience with his brother Eliab apply to you or members of your family? What is really quite human about the problems David faced with his brother? What did he do to meet those problems? How much of his method can you adapt to your situation?
2. What gigantic challenges do you face? Are they in any respect like Goliath in defying the God you are learning to know personally? What are some successful ways to meet those challenges?

3.

4.

PUTTING THIS LESSON INTO ACTION

1. From your local library or bookstore obtain biographies of Christian missionaries, athletes, and others who have faced challenges in the name of God. Make several of these available to specific members of your class, asking them to read and report soon to the rest of the class. A good way to get students reading is for you to begin the first chapter of a book, reading it aloud to the class until you reach an interesting point; then break off and give it to someone in the class to take and read.
2. The story of David and Goliath is often referred to whenever an underdog is victorious—a small college team defeats a major university, an unknown candidate upsets a political big-shot, a seemingly helpless nation defends itself against an aggressor. Two or three students might do some research into several examples from sports, politics, and international affairs and present reports to the class. Discuss the factors which lead to the surprising defeat of the larger and more powerful by the small and weak. What is the basic principle here?

LESSON 4

1 Samuel 18

1 SAMUEL 18: READ ALOUD

WHAT DOES IT SAY? WHAT DOES IT MEAN?

1. Why does Saul wish to keep David in his service?

Initially, of course, Saul wants David present for the purpose of celebrating his victory and capitalizing on the improved morale of his army; furthermore, he must fulfill his promise and honor the hero with his reward. But the larger reason is the quickly developed friendship between Saul's son Jonathan and David. Exactly what Saul's motives are can only be guessed at. Perhaps he loved Jonathan enough to want his every wish satisfied; perhaps he recognized immediately the threat to Jonathan's succession as king and wished to have Jonathan recognize it too. Until the victory song and its insult to Saul, the narrative gives us no reason to suppose any animosity towards David.

2. What do Jonathan's gifts to David represent in their friendship?

   What does David give to Jonathan in return?

Jonathan's gifts of clothing and weapons are a token of giving himself completely. In return, David offers nothing tangible—what can a shepherd give a prince? We are to assume that friendship and loyalty of themselves were a sufficient prize for Jonathan. Students may be aware of the perversion of this relationship into an argument for homosexuality; obviously nothing in the text supports that argument. On the contrary, students should be encouraged to know that our language is full of phrases that speak of friendship on its own terms: bosom companion, friend that sticks closer than a brother, even best friend.

Poetic Parallelism

3. What does the women's victory song mean?

What effect does it have on Saul?

As Saul's army returns from the battlefront, the troops are greeted by exultant civilians. Students may recall "ticker tape" parades for various celebrities—astronauts, athletes, and others; or perhaps a pep rally for a school team led by cheerleaders. In this case the king takes second place to the new hero David. On the surface the song praises David's immediate accomplishment, but Saul takes it to be a permanent threat to his security as monarch. He believes the song will put grandiose ideas into David's head; so from that time on, Saul eyes David warily and jealously.

4. How does Saul's jealousy of David show itself?

How does Saul attempt to get rid of David?

Application

How does our jealousy affect the way we view what other people are doing?

Saul relapses into the evil mood of paranoia and persecution complex discussed earlier. Once again, David plays and sings to soothe Saul. But twice Saul throws a spear at David, intending to kill him. His failure at such close range convinces Saul that the Lord has now chosen David over himself. Instead of submitting to God's sovereignty, Saul tries to have David killed in battle; but because "the Lord was with him," David is always successful.

5. How does Saul use his daughters in plotting against David?

Cultural Context

What marriage customs does this passage describe?

Saul uses his daughters like pawns to win a chess match. The king has already promised a princess to the hero who will take on Goliath. It is accepted in that culture that the princess in question would have no choice in the matter. Now in fulfilling his promise, Saul adds a condition: David is to receive the oldest daughter as his wife only if he will replace Saul in fighting "the battles of the Lord" (verse 17). In other words, the daughter Merab is no longer a reward for killing Goliath; she has become a property negotiated as part of a deal in which Saul seeks to protect himself from death in war while guaranteeing David's death. However, Merab isn't available when the time for marriage comes; she is already engaged or married to someone else. Her sister Michal, however, is in love with David and willing to take Merab's place. Their father Saul doesn't care who marries David, just so his plans aren't thwarted. Marriage customs of the time disregarded any rights of women for choice or love. It is only mere coincidence that Michal happens to marry a man she already loves. In ancient societies often the bridegroom had to pay for the privilege of marrying the bride: Laban demanded fourteen years of work from Jacob for Rachel.

6. How does Saul's demand demonstrate the barbarism of the time?

How well does David meet Saul's demand?

Is he bloodthirsty or a showoff?

Saul's demand is an indication of his barbarity. He orders David to bring back evidence that he has killed and then mutilated 100 Philistines. This is similar, although not comparable, to an American Indian chief's demand for enemy scalps. The fact that David doubles Saul's requirement shows Saul how invulnerable David has become. This fact increases Saul's hatred and fear, making them permanent.

7. What decision does Saul reach as a result of David's success?

How does arriving at that decision affect Saul's attitude?

What do verses 28 and 29 show about human nature?

Truth-principle

Foolish Saul, instead of finally recognizing that he is no match for the will of God, insists on carrying out his feud with David to the bitter end. *Bitter* becomes the key word to describe Saul's condition. For Saul there can be no remedy from his inner anguish until he acknowledges God's sovereign right to rule through whomever he chooses. Saul prefers to sulk. The Philistines also seem not to have learned anything from David's victory over Goliath. They persist in sending out their challengers, most of whom David defeats personally. Persistence in wretchedness is a dominant human characteristic among sinful people who choose not to repent.

Narrative Techniques

8. You may want to discuss the way that

summary paragraphs are interspersed between specific incidents and dialogue both in this chapter and in chapter 19 as well. Students may want to consider chronology and duration of the struggles between Saul and David. The *Zondervan Pictorial Encyclopedia of the Bible* article, "Chronology of the Old Testament" has helpful information.

HOW DOES THIS APPLY TO ME?

1. What does it mean to *have* a friend? What does it mean to *be* a friend? Encourage the students to draw up a list of traits they hope to find in their friends. Let each one determine for himself which traits he possesses.
2. What does it mean to be jealous of somebody else? Encourage honesty in examining the causes of jealousy as well as its poisonous effects. What actions or attitudes can help root out jealousy before it becomes destructive?
3.
4.

PUTTING THIS LESSON INTO ACTION

1. Invite members of the class to write a personal letter to a friend, thanking him for the qualities of character that make the friendship important. This letter will be private.
2. Suggest that some members of the class make a survey of local gift shops or other stores where greeting cards for friends are sold. Let each participant in this activity bring to class one or two cards to display and explain the symbols of friendship illustrating the card and the terms of friendship in which its greeting is expressed.
3. What kinds of gifts do friends give each other today? Let members of the class inquire among classmates, parents, or others to discover what our society considers appropriate tokens of friendship as distinct from more intimate tokens of family relationships.

LESSON 5

1 Samuel 20; Psalm 34

BACKGROUND TO 1 SAMUEL 20

This is the first lesson to break away from the chapter-by-chapter sequence. If your class is assigned to read the entire text containing the narratives about David (1 Samuel 16–1 Kings 2:12), you will no doubt wish to question them about intervening chapters as they occur. If your class is reading only the chapters assigned in these lessons, you will probably wish to summarize the action.

In 1 Samuel 19, Saul finally shows that he is a premeditating murderer. His previous attacks on David (1 Sam. 18:10–11) could have been spontaneous; now, however, he openly discusses his hatred with Jonathan and others at court. Jonathan keeps faith with his friend David and warns him; Jonathan also promises to keep David informed of impending danger.

But clearly Jonathan is also a faithful son. He loves and respects his father; he doesn't wish to see his father destroy himself with hatred, and for no cause. Jonathan reasons with Saul, showing him how needless his hatred of David is, how undeserving of death David is. Saul apparently is moved by his son's argument and swears an oath by the Lord that David no longer has anything to fear. Then Jonathan tells David the good news, and David returns to his home (presumably near Saul's court in Gibeah) to live with his wife Michal, Saul's daughter.

An uncertain amount of time passes during which David once again leads Saul's army against the Philistines and is victorious. But a third time Saul is overcome by evil and tries to kill David with his spear. Returning home to Michal, David listens to her loving warning to escape immediately. She places her household idols in David's bed to create a dummy. When Saul's assassins arrive to kill David, she lies to them, telling them that David is sick, so they return to Saul. He knows his daughter and distrusts her. The killers are sent back with orders to bring the sick man—bed and all—into his presence, where he will personally kill him. Saul's goons find the dummy in the bed and take Michal to answer to her father. Again she lies, showing that although her motivation or intentions were honorable in attempting to save her husband's life, Michal's human weakness was insufficient to withstand her father's anger. Later Michal is married to another man (1 Sam. 25:44), and David also takes several other wives. Michal has no child to stand in the royal succession (see 2 Samuel 6:23), so Saul's descendants do not ascend the throne by any means.

The final paragraph in chapter 19 relates how, even in the frenzy of his hatred, Saul is subject to the supernatural power of God to frustrate his pursuit of David and render him helpless. Prophesying meant speaking for God; it sometimes was accompanied by physical manifestations such as lying in a certain position (see Ezekiel 4).

Chapter 20 resumes the narrative with David's next-to-last meeting with Jonathan. Students should be reminded of God's requirements for particular rituals. According to Numbers 28 and 29, God commanded Moses to instruct the Israelites regarding weekly, monthly, seasonal, and annual observances. These festivals were a means of giving thanks to God for sustaining life and providing care. On this particular occasion the new moon observance appears to coincide with some special annual celebration which might reasonably demand David's attendance at home. It is presented to Saul as a family obligation, with David submitting to the natural authority of his brother, presumably Eliab. If Saul were at all reasonable, he would surely understand David's excuse. An additional note: Ritual observance required purification. If anyone should be found ritually unclean, according to the law of God given to Moses (see Leviticus 7:20–21), he must not take part in any sacred feast until he has been forgiven and cleansed. Thus Saul assumes that David's first absence is caused by ritual necessity to cleanse himself.

1 SAMUEL 20: READ ALOUD

WHAT DOES IT SAY? WHAT DOES IT MEAN?

Dialogue

1. How does this episode reflect the three main characters?

Consider the extensive use of direct quotation. The words used and the insight expressed help us to understand this episode as a high point in the relationship between David and Jonathan.

2. From the questions David asks Jonathan, what can you tell about David's state of mind at this time?

Clearly, David is in an agitated state of mind. He has had to run for his life, leaving his home, and seeking safety and advice from Samuel. David is in no mood for "sweet talk" or comforting words that lack evidence to support them. He wants to know where he stands. Jonathan must be assumed to be sincere, but he is either unusually naive about his father's character, unwarrantedly optimistic over the possibilities of reconciliation, or else simply unwilling to face the dangerous realities of David's situation. Jonathan shows himself to be an unlikely candidate for kingship: his inability to judge a serious human conflict would have been his downfall in short order. David is much more realistic. He sees how close he is to death—only a step! He refuses to return to Saul's court until he has tested the king's feelings.

Plot

3. How does David plan to confirm once and for all Saul's feelings toward him?

If Saul is unreasonable about David's absence from the ceremonial observance of the new

moon, David knows his course. Questions
may arise about David's scheme to test Saul.
It's obviously not true that David has gone to
Bethlehem, not true that his brother has or-
dered him to appear (see verse 29); furthermore, David is requiring Jonathan to tell
these lies. Several suggested responses:
David isn't perfect or sinless, nor does the
Bible present him as a perfect model in all his
actions. Lying may be permitted in military
confrontations such as spying, and Saul is
David's enemy (1 Sam. 18:29). On this difficult point, however, you will want to avoid
becoming trapped in the indiscriminate
"end-justifies-the-means" argument.

Plot

4. What is Jonathan's plan for informing
   David of his safety or danger?

   *How does Jonathan's responsibility to
   his father fit in with his promise to his
   friend?*

Jonathan agrees to David's plan to absent
himself from Saul's feast. When the king's
reaction is known, Jonathan will go to the
field where David is hiding and by a pre-
arranged verbal signal or code give David the
message. "This side" means safety; "beyond"
means grave danger. By directing the boy to
find the arrows, Jonathan is really saying to
David, "Come out of hiding and join me" or
"Run for your life." Jonathan as an adult has
a commitment to God; he knows David has
been chosen as the next king.

5. What happens at Saul's new moon festival?

   *What is Saul's real reason for hating
   David?*

   *How does Saul show himself to be a
   maniac?*

Saul sits in his usual seat, next to the wall—

perhaps an indication of his paranoia. Saul notices David's empty place. Students who have read *Macbeth* will possibly notice a similarity in Macbeth's statement about Banquo's absence from his dinner. On the first occasion—apparently these festivals spanned three evening meals—Saul assumes that David's absence has a legitimate cause in ritual purification. On the second evening, however, he angrily inquires and receives Jonathan's answer. Instead of accepting his son's response, Saul turns his anger against Jonathan. Saul also reveals the deepest reason for his hating David. Knowing that God has removed his blessing from Saul, the king is also certain that his own line of sons will never succeed him. He tries to use family pride to undermine Jonathan's friendship with David. He knows, or at least suspects, that Jonathan is protecting David, and he then orders Jonathan to turn David over to him. When Jonathan protests, Saul's murderous nature turns upon his own son. Jonathan needs no further convincing that David can never safely return.

6. What are the most important features of David and Jonathan's friendship?

Kind of Language

   What are the terms by which they pledge their word to each other?

Students should be encouraged to draw out of the text specific words and phrases which show personal affection and respect as well as an everlasting bond of mutual concern between their posterity. Someone in the class might know and recall—or be encouraged to read about—Jonathan's crippled son Mephibosheth (see 2 Samuel 9). Similarly, students should note the various words and phrases: "God forbid" (KJV), "as the Lord lives and as you live," "may the Lord deal with me, be it ever so severely," or in KVJ, "the Lord do so and much more unto me," and so on. These are solemn phrases, not flippant, idle words from careless mouths. They are spoken in deep earnestness about matters of life and death, with God himself called as witness to the sincerity of the speaker's vows.

BACKGROUND TO PSALM 34

Following his painful parting from Jonathan, David entered on a decade of life as a fugitive, often in exile. On occasion he even sought refuge among his supposedly worst enemies, the Philistines (see 1 Samuel 21:10–15). Once, to protect himself, he pretended to be a lunatic, groveling in the streets and drooling like an infant. Observe the inscription before Psalm 34 which refers to this incident. Abimelech may be the title of Achish. The Philistine king saw David's strange behavior and instead of killing him, as his advisers urged, the Philistine simply told David to move on. So David's life was spared by abasing himself and, as this song of praise shows, by his unswerving trust in the Lord.

The psalm seems to be divided into two sections: In verses 1–10 the speaker expresses praise; in 11–22 he addresses himself to an audience he calls "my children," giving them instruction based upon his own experience.

PSALM 34: READ ALOUD

WHAT DOES IT SAY? WHAT DOES IT MEAN?

Denotation   1. Songs are written for various reasons—to express love, to rouse patriotic feelings, to accompany hard work, to tell a sad story. In verse 1, what is the songwriter's declared purpose for Psalm 34?

Not only in verse 1, but also in verses 2 and 3, the songwriter clearly declares his purpose to be praise of God, thanksgiving to him, and exaltation or glorification of the name of the Lord. Students should be encouraged to differentiate among the several terms—"extol," "praise," "magnify," or "glorify," and "exalt"—the psalmist uses. A dictionary for definitions and a concordance for other uses in the Bible will be helpful.

Connotation

2. Assuming that David is the songwriter, what is important about the singer's expression of praise "at all times" or "continually" ("no matter what happens," LB)?

Application

How do my circumstances shape my attitude? (Consider Philippians 4:11–13.)

This is a song born out of great hardship, personal danger, humiliation, and heartbreaking loss of friend and family. Yet it is also a song of deliverance, which means it is a song of hope. David is the great example of one who recognizes hope in every act of God; therefore, praise is an ongoing obligation because God is always—"at all times"—at work on our behalf. Anyone can give thanks for deliverance, but David urges the same spirit of praise and thanksgiving even in the middle of the problem. Because he practices what he preaches, he is a worthy model.

Theme

3. In the first three verses, what is the theme of this victory song?

David disallows any bragging about his own skills or bravery. The Lord deserves all the credit. "The humble" ought to include anyone with a clear idea of who God is. Once we come to understand who God is, how can we be anything but humble? Therefore, praising God doesn't rob any of us of the headlines; praising God simply puts the praise where it belongs. Part of knowing God is rejoicing in anything that honors him, which is why "the humble" are glad to listen to David's song. If you don't enjoy hearing God praised, you've identified yourself as one of those who doesn't acknowledge him as Lord. Any student who can speak about the contrast between a praiseworthy God and the humble singer will understand the theme.

Figurative Language

4. In verses 4–10, how does the singer describe and contrast his previous and present conditions?

What terms does he use to support his earlier statements, attributing praise to God rather than to himself?

Explain the military figure of speech in verse 7.

What is the relationship between tasting *and* trusting (KJV) *in verse 8?*

What does the singer mean when he urges his listener to fear *the Lord?*

Contrast

Who are "the lions" in verse 10? How do they contrast with those who "seek the Lord"?

Students who read this passage carefully will discover that the speaker's previous condition included:

- separation from God, yet within calling distance (verse 4)
- bondage to fear, from which deliverance was desired (verse 4)
- poverty or wretchedness, mostly caused by a variety of "troubles" (verse 6)

The speaker's present condition includes:

- deliverance from fears and troubles (verses 4, 6)
- the security of being protected by the

guardian angel, like a sentry (verse 7)

- provision of blessings that are pleasing (verse 8)
- provision of needs (verse 9)

This series of contrasts is summed up with the figurative language of verse 10. "Lions" ought to be capable of providing for themselves through their strength, speed, and superiority; yet they are described, by contrast to the singer, as lacking food, being famished. The singer has none of the physical prowess of the animal, only trust in the Lord. This is sufficient to provide every need.

Voice

5. In verse 11, what role does the singer now assume?

On what basis does he presume to teach?

What will be his lesson?

Who are his pupils?

The text clearly indicates the role of teacher taken on by someone who has learned through personal experience the benefits of fearing God. This is his lesson to pupils whom he calls "my children." At the time of this psalm, David himself had no sons and daughters; "my children" may be his followers who came to him at the Cave of Adullam (see 1 Samuel 22:1–2), including his brothers. In this sense the word would almost be ironic. Can you see Eliab as one of David's *children?* Yet anyone who has only just begun to learn what David has to teach is a spiritual child. Of course, it's also possible that the phrase, "my children," is a later addition, a poetic revision by the author at a time when he had children of his own to whom he wished to sing this advice, which applies to anyone desiring a long life.

Truth-
principle

Irony

6. Summarize the lesson given in verses 13–14.

> *What is ironic about this teacher's urging his pupils to "seek power and pursue it"?*

Students should be encouraged to spend ample time with each of the parts of these verses: speech as an indicator of right living; action as an indicator of right living; peace as a goal for right living. Obviously it's ironic— although not hypocritical—for a man of war to urge peace. Students should be encouraged to recognize that every sane soldier would prefer peace to war; soldiers fight wars to achieve peace, unless their motives are entirely evil.

Contrast

7. In verses 15–22, how do the righteous and unrighteous differ?

> *According to verses 19–22, what specific blessings do the righteous enjoy that are not available to the unrighteous?*

> *What assurance does the singer offer to the righteous, even after death?*

Verses 15 and 16 make the contrast clear; God watches over the righteous, keeping a loving eye on them, listening for their cry of need; but God is here pictured as turning his face away from the unrighteous, leaving them, it seems, to the consequences of their own wickedness. The contrast is again implied in verse 17, with the unrighteous' refusal to call on God for help left to the reader's ability to read between the lines. This cry for help must be accompanied by "a broken heart" and "a contrite spirit" (KJV). In other words, repentance is necessary to become righteous. However, the righteous aren't automatically spared life's natural calamities, and it's never to be assumed that life's natural disasters have overtaken us because of sin. Sin may be at the bottom of certain catastrophes, but illness, death, flood, fire, and loss in other ways are part of the human experience. How then are the righteous any better off than the unrighteous? God provides deliverance and the grace to sustain these natural disasters (see 1 Corinthians 10:13). The righteous never need to feel abandoned or "desolate." Furthermore, the promise is that the Lord's servants will be redeemed, a promise pointing to eternal union with God.

HOW DOES THIS APPLY TO ME?

1. As in 1 Samuel 18, David's friendship with Jonathan seems to be his one source of human comfort, now that he is no longer safe at home with his wife. What are our obligations to a friend who is having difficulties at home? How are we supposed to help someone who may even be in danger at home?
2. What responsibility, if any, do we have for a friend's family after the friend has moved away or died? Is our commitment to the friend alone?
3. Psalm 34 seems to speak quite a bit about how we use our mouths and tongues. What's important about our speech? How much does what we say define who we are? To what extent does our character determine our speech?
4. How do verses 9 and 10 of Psalm 34 relate to me? Do I feel a lack of some particular thing? If I do, is it because my attitude toward God is not right? Or is it because the thing would not be good for me?

5.

6.

PUTTING THIS LESSON INTO ACTION

1. Write a brief account of a narrow escape you have had from danger. Or write a song or poem about the experience. Let your reader see or feel with you the relief you feel after the danger is past.
2. Discuss with your parents or other family members what arrangements they have made for people to care for their children in the event of the parents' death. Why have they chosen these persons to care for their children?
3. Discuss your school rules on disciplinary action for use of profane language. What is the basis for judging unacceptable language? Why does the school administer the punishment it does? How effective is that punishment? What is the real root of any problem with profane language? Write a recommendation to the student government and school administration based on your discussion of disciplinary action for language abuse.

1 Samuel 24; Psalm 57

BACKGROUND

David leaves Gath, where he had pretended lunacy in order to save his life, and goes into the wilderness south of Bethlehem. That region is pockmarked with caves in the ravines. Unless one knows the terrain, it can be a dangerous area to explore, and it would make a perfect place for a fugitive to hide. Soon David collects around him a group of renegades like himself. Throughout these chapters there is a wealth of geographic detail. Make sure students are continuing to use maps to follow the action.

In 1 Samuel 22 and 23, the narrator tells of Saul's futile and vengeful efforts to track down David; his desperation carries him to the extreme of murdering Abimelech, the priest of God, and all other priests in the sacred city of Nob. Still Saul is unable to capture David because God continues to preserve him (1 Sam. 23:14).

But Jonathan finds David—no doubt with the help of those who know the abiding friendship between these two men. In frank and open terms, Jonathan commits himself to acknowledging David as the Lord's choice to succeed Saul; he expresses his willingness to serve David (1 Sam. 23:16-18).

Once again Saul pursues David, and this time nearly catches him. But just as he is closing in, a message arrives that the Philistines have chosen this time of Saul's distraction to attack. So Saul has to make a choice: he chooses to defend the kingdom against the Philistines and leaves David for another time.

The episode in 1 Samuel 24 follows immediately; Psalm 57 is identified in its heading as belonging to this episode. Current scholarship identifies "Selah" as a musical notation, such as *tutti,* meaning "all instruments" play. At these places in the psalms, there may have been instrumental interludes.

At this lesson midway through the course of study, you should make up your own questions, based on what you have discovered about the kind of help your students need. You should also encourage your students to read 1 Samuel 24 and write down several questions in the *What Does It Say? What Does It Mean?* categories. Both Saul and David have appeared in previous lessons; how are their actions consistent with what has already been presented?

Have members of the class hand in their questions so that you can see how well they understand this question and answer method. How will they use their skills in their future Bible study? Do they grasp that their aim is to achieve the skill not of answering someone else's questions, but of framing their own and of applying principles based on the information learned from the Scriptures?

1 SAMUEL 24: READ ALOUD

WHAT DOES IT SAY? WHAT DOES IT MEAN?

First Samuel 24 is a brief, tightly compact story, dense with human interest, irony, wretched remorse, and a confession that does not result in repentance. Students should be commended if their questions disclose some of these elements of the story:

- David's continual need to run for his life
- Saul's source of information in supporters who were always ready to turn David over to him, presumably to collect a reward
- David's regard for Saul as lawful ruler because he is "the Lord's anointed" (Observe the differences in their attitudes on this point.)
- David's sensitive conscience
- David's plea to Saul, including the old adage, "From evil-doers come evil deeds"
- David's characterization of himself as worthless, no more than a dead dog or a flea
- Saul's emotional distress and confession of wrongdoing
- Saul's acknowledgment of God's providence in sending him into that cave where David might demonstrate mercy and love

- Saul's recognition of David as God's inevitable choice to be king
- Saul's request that David not exterminate his family
- Saul's apparent inability to progress from his remorse or confession of guilt to repentance, including the specific intent to change one's actions

PSALM 57: READ ALOUD

WHAT DOES IT SAY? WHAT DOES IT MEAN?

Psalm 57 may have been written before the incident in 1 Samuel 24, in which case the words of Saul would have seemed like a temporary answer to the prayer of verse 1. If the psalm was written after this incident, David at least has cause for hope that, indeed, his present "calamities" or "storms" may soon be over. Students should be commended if their questions reveal their awareness of

- David's intense reliance on God, like a new-hatched bird's reliance on the mother's wings
- God's sovereignty, omnipotence, glory; but most of all, his mercy
- David's use of metaphors: wings, weapons, snares, and traps
- David's sense that what people say is a threat to him, perhaps as much as Saul's sword
- David's pleasure in making music in praise of God

HOW DOES THIS APPLY TO ME?

1. How does the adage in 1 Samuel 24:13 hold true? How is one evil followed by another as I try to cover up a wrong?
2. What steps should be taken to make sure that feelings of remorse or guilt lead directly to a change of mind or repentance? We know that God continues to forgive us, but at the same time we are not to go on sinning so that grace may abound (see Romans 6). How often, then, can we expect to be forgiven?

3.

4.

PUTTING THIS LESSON INTO ACTION

1. Discuss the relationship between an individual person, a Christian, a school, or a church and the government under which it operates. Does David's respect for the king's person reveal a truth-principle to follow? Interview pastors or school administrators to find out their ideas.
2. Does a Christian have the right of self-defense? Perhaps members of the class could debate this issue.

LESSON 7

1 Samuel 28

BACKGROUND TO 1 SAMUEL 28

In spite of Saul's confession of wrongdoing against David (see 1 Samuel 24:16–21), David remains a fugitive until long after Saul's death. Chapters 25–27 relate three incidents in David's continuing flight to avoid Saul's killing him.

In chapter 25, the narrator offers a romantic interlude in the otherwise bloody story. Abigail, wife of the mean-spirited Nabal, shows herself to be an independent woman, as wise as she is said to be beautiful. Her petition on behalf of her husband, in spite of his refusal to help David, spares his life temporarily. But even her goodness cannot protect him from the effects of greed. When he learns of what she has given David to save Nabal from David's revenge, he has a seizure and dies. Having been faithful to her first husband, Abigail the widow is now free to marry David. This story makes an interesting counterbalance to the later instance of David's sin with Bathsheba.

Students may be curious or troubled about polygamy in the Bible. Mosaic law forbids adultery and fornication but has nothing to say about polygamy as such. It appears that whereas a husband might have several (or even many) wives, no woman could have more than one husband. The principle is the man's responsibility to care for the woman; Mosaic law does not permit loose relationships. The Christian church in the New Testament did not permit polygamous members to hold office (see 1 Timothy 3:1–13, for instance).

First Samuel 26 recalls the incident in chapter 24; once more David finds Saul within his power to kill and spares him because he is "the Lord's anointed." Clearly David's understanding of this favored status allows no taking of matters into his own hands. Saul is God's man until God removes him.

In this incident, as in chapter 24, Saul expresses shame for his murderous attitude toward David; but here he pledges never again to harm David, a pledge David cannot believe. Students may be interested in the phenomenon of remorse, the feeling of guilt which sweeps over a person and causes him to utter vows of reformation, "turning over a new leaf," and so on. Yet when the stimulus to remorse is past, the old bitterness often returns in increased measure. Remorse and repentance are two different reactions. Remorse means feeling bad because of one's sin; repentance means actively seeking forgiveness for one's sin and determining not to repeat it.

.Realizing how untrustworthy Saul is, David decides to keep on the run. In chapter 27, he flees once again to his former enemies the Philistines, to the very king before whom he had earlier pretended lunacy (see 1 Samuel 21:10–15). By now David's reputation is so great that Achish is glad to have him, as a renegade, on the Philistines' side. Achish supposes that David has burned his bridges behind him and can never return to Israel: but Achish doesn't know God's intentions for David.

Students may well be puzzled by David's decision to live among the mortal enemies of God's people. You might remind them that this story is not intended to be a perfect moral example in all its parts; David makes mistakes for which he pays dearly. Trusting himself and his followers to the Philistines was one of those mistakes—perhaps a prudent-seeming move at the time but at root an act of desperation resulting from lack of faith in the God who had protected him thus far. Living among the enemy as one of them would mean that sooner or later David would have to fight with the enemy against God's people. In perspective, it is also true that during this time David was making war on some groups of Canaanites whom God had commanded the Israelites to wipe out, including the Amalekites whom Saul was supposed to have destroyed.

1 SAMUEL 28: READ ALOUD

WHAT DOES IT SAY? WHAT DOES IT MEAN?

Cause-Effect   1. What are the consequences of David's decision to live among the Philistines?

When the enemies of Israel make war against his own people, David is forced to demonstrate his new loyalty by fighting against Israel. What Achish demands of David, as proof of his new loyalty, is similar to tests of spiritual loyalty: In Japan, in the seventeenth and eighteenth centuries, Roman Catholics were arrested and forced to spit or trample on the crucifix; refusal to do so meant death. Some interpreters argue that David never intended to fight his own people, that he was duping Achish into trusting him so that he could turn on the Philistines, just as their commanders feared (see 1 Samuel 29:3–11). But if this were so, why did David accept Achish's reluctant concession to his commanders? Why did David leave the battle and return home? It seems that David intended to fight Israel and was prevented from doing so by suspicious Philistine commanders. Of course, in the overall picture of David's life, the Philistines did David a favor by not allowing him to fight his own people.

2. What is Saul's reaction to the new Philistine threat?

Does he know that David is part of the opposing army?

Why is Saul so stricken with fear?

For several years now Saul has reigned as king in complete knowledge that God has rejected him. Every battle is a threat to his personal safety, for although Saul has been disobedient to God and murderous toward David, Saul has never lost his sense of God's sovereignty. This impending battle is particularly frightening to him. The text does not reveal whether or not Saul knew David's whereabouts, but it's not unlikely he did; he received information about David in other instances. David's presence is not a factor in Saul's fright, however; he is dismayed by several things: the size of the Philistine army, the failure of his priests to find any consolation from God, and the recent death of Samuel, taking from Saul his last hope for reconciliation with God.

Irony

3. Why is it ironic that Saul decides to seek a medium to tell his fortune?

   Why does he go to her in disguise?

   Why is the woman afraid before she recognizes Saul and terrified after she recognizes him?

Students should be disturbed by this whole incident, especially since it appears to place the souls of the dead at the disposal of mediums. As a beginning point in discussion, direct students to various passages in the Bible condemning and warning against all forms of occult consultation (see Exodus 22:18, Leviticus 19:31, Deuteronomy 18:10, and Nahum 3:4). Significantly, God condemns witchcraft and "familiar spirits" not because they are the work of fraud and charlatans but because they are *real!* Students need to be encouraged to understand the Bible's teaching on spirit-life: Evil is a fact which infests those who submit to its power. The Bible is also clear in attributing certain supernatural occurrences to the power of witches, magicians, sorcerers, and so forth (see Exodus 7:8–13, Acts 8:9–24). But in these cases and others, God's supreme power over evil also demonstrates itself. After Samuel's death, Saul, who banned all mediums and other occultists, feels the loss of the prophet who was his means of access to God. He grows so desperate that he becomes willing to break his own law and the law of God in order to find some comfort for the future. He goes to the woman at Endor in disguise to protect his reputation and honor, as though these depended on public opinion! The woman is continuing in her occult trade in spite of Saul's ban—an indication of what happens when governments try to legislate sin out of existence: it merely goes into hiding. When she is approached about practicing her evil work, she is surprised and afraid to have been discovered by strangers. But she grows terrified when the form of Samuel does appear, as the woman sees that she has unwittingly become a participant in God's divine judgment on Saul.

Interpretation   4. If God forbids witchcraft and the occult, why is the woman able to summon up Samuel from the dead?

The Bible teaches that God is a personal deity who works with individuals in particular ways. He does not generally and universally cause walls to collapse when trumpets blow or ocean-going passengers to be swallowed whole by great fish. But in particular instances he intervenes, even using such people as the Egyptian pharaoh, Samson, and the witch at Endor to do his bidding. In this case—and this is not to be taken as a spiritual principle but as a historical exception—God speaks a horrifying message in a horrifying manner. He gives Saul what Saul thinks he wants, that is, another chance to communicate with Samuel. But the witch herself has no power to summon Samuel unless God permits.

Dramatic Technique   5. What is Samuel's message to Saul? How is it given?

Why is Saul doomed? Where will he go?

After Samuel has protested against Saul's en-gaging in witchcraft, he names the Lord as Saul's enemy and asks why Saul should be interested in what Samuel might tell him; in other words, Samuel is saying, "Saul, why bother to ask? You know what you're going to hear is condemnation." Furthermore, Samuel reminds Saul that he already knows every-thing Samuel might tell him; Samuel's prophecy and the sign of the torn cloak (see 1 Samuel 15:26–28) have been fulfilled. All this is God's retribution for Saul's disobedience in sparing the Amalekites. Furthermore—and this probably is what Saul most and least wanted to hear!—in the next day's battle Saul and his sons will be killed. Interestingly, Samuel specifies that Saul and his sons will be "with me" (verse 19). This phrase may refer to the state of being dead—that is, "with me in death"—or to a specific location—"with me in Sheol," the presumed resting place of souls awaiting eternal judgment which would then lead to the presence of God or separation from God (see various ref-erences, including Psalms 6:5, 16:10, 31:17, 55:15, 86:13, and 139:8; also Isaiah 38:10).

According to the second account of this nar-rative (see 1 Chronicles 10:13–14), Saul was doomed not only for his disobedience with the Amalekites but also for his very act of seeking out the witch. In other words, God allowed Saul his wish but made him pay the consequences of his sin. The narrator in 1 Chronicles raises a problem, however, when he says that Saul consulted the witch instead of the Lord. Doesn't 1 Samuel 38:6 say that Saul prayed and the Lord refused to answer? Perhaps the problem can be resolved in this light: None of Saul's prayers can be answered until he wholly and absolutely repents of his past and present sins, which means ending his hatred of David and resigning himself to God's plan for David to succeed him. As long as Saul persists in attempting to thwart God by killing David, God has deaf ears to Saul's prayers (Ps. 66:18).

Note the dramatic style of this section: the woman's fright, the spirit's questions and his message repeating earlier communication from God, with the climax—tomorrow you will die and your army will be defeated—followed by the denouement as the woman deals with Saul's physical hunger.

6. How do Saul and the woman react to Samuel's message?

Saul is so overcome by shock and fear that he falls on the ground. But it is of no avail; the spirit of Samuel has departed, and his message of disaster will not be retracted. Saul's grief has come too late. He is also suffering from lack of food, which has weakened his body. The woman tries to help him, but her comfort does not extend to his spiritual needs. She does what she can to encourage him, killing the "fatted calf" (see Luke 15:23) and making some bread for Saul and his men.

Students who have read or seen a production of Shakespeare's *Macbeth* may enjoy discussing the playwright's borrowing from this story. In Act IV, scene 1, Macbeth goes to inquire of the Weird Sisters or witches. From them he learns the equivocal prophecies of his impending death and succession by a line of kings other than his own descendants. Similarly in *Moby-Dick*, Captain Ahab consults a worshiper of the occult named Fedallah and receives veiled prophecies of death.

HOW DOES THIS APPLY TO ME?

1. For many years modern society treated the existence of a spirit world as a joke or a carnival fraud, but no more. What is today's attitude? How have books, films, and other popular media contributed to a new fascination with the occult?
2. Why does God expressly forbid consulting fortunetellers, mediums, and other occultists?
3. What can Christians in North America do when a store dealing in occult arts opens in a shopping center? What are their rights under the law? What are the merchant's rights under the law?

4.

5.

PUTTING THIS LESSON INTO ACTION

1. As a teacher you should try to be aware of what interests or involvements your students have with occult practices. You should help them to consider biblical prohibitions and discuss with them the ways that even things which look harmless, such as newspaper horoscopes, can lead to other areas. Encourage them to discuss why they like to read horoscopes since many are ambiguous. Do they really want to know the future? Are not God's guidelines given in the Scriptures enough for us?
2. Missionaries and other travelers to distant places sometimes report having seen evidence of occult or spirit-world activity hostile to the Bible's teaching. Consult your pastor or a visiting missionary and ask for information he may have on this subject. Or read one of the following books or chapters:

> Dolphin, Lambert. *Astrology, Occultism and the Drug Culture.* Westchester, Ill.: Good News, 1970.
> Guinness, Os. *The Dust of Death.* Chapter 8: "Encircling Eyes." Downers Grove, Ill.: InterVarsity, 1973.
> Kerr, John Stevens. *The Mystery and Magic of the Occult.* Philadelphia: Fortress, 1971.

Lockerbie, D. Bruce. *The Cosmic Center.* Chapter 3: "Scare-crows among Cucumbers." Grand Rapids: Eerdmans, 1977.

Martin, Walter R. *Kingdom of the Occult.* Tapes.

Montgomery, John Warwick. *Principalities and Powers.* Minneapolis: Bethany, 1973.

Petersen, William J. *Those Curious New Cults.* New Canaan, Conn.: Keats, 1973.

Unger, Merrill F. *Biblical Demonology.* Wheaton, Ill.: Victor, 1952.

3. If a student were told, as Saul was, that he was going to die the next day, what would he do? Many people who are terminally ill have to make these decisions. How should a person comfort someone who does know that he is dying?

LESSON 8

Psalm 18

BACKGROUND

The headnote to this psalm identifies it as having been written soon after David's accession to the throne of Israel, in accord with Samuel's prophecy. As such, it is the king's own hymn of praise to God for all his protection and blessing through, perhaps, a dozen years or more of danger.

Saul is dead, Jonathan is dead (1 Sam. 31); David, who had planned to fight with the Philistines against Saul (1 Sam. 29), has been dismissed as untrustworthy and has returned home to Ziklag only to discover that the Amalekites have attacked in his absence (1 Sam. 30). The city has been destroyed, but God graciously allows David to recover his family and all their belongings safely. Nonetheless, David must know how dearly he has paid for his disloyalty to his own people in joining forces with the very enemy he had long ago accused of defying the Lord of hosts.

From this experience David states a principle of generosity which continues to be observed in some enterprises to this day—the right of even the most insignificant participant to share in the benefits (see 1 Samuel 30:24). David also shows prudence in sending back to his friends among the elders of Judah portions of the spoils he has taken from the enemy.

Then David learns of Saul and Jonathan's deaths, and his sorrow breaks into a song of lamentation (2 Sam. 1). After his mourning, David leaves Ziklag and the Philistines and goes to Hebron; there he is anointed king by some who wish to have him reign. But there is a rival claim by Ish-Bosheth, one of Saul's sons. Civil war breaks out in all its violence and treachery (2 Sam. 2–4). After seven-and-a-half years, David is crowned king of Israel (2 Sam. 5:1–3), and his reign over the whole country begins, with his headquarters in Jerusalem which becomes known as "the city of David."

Psalm 18 also appears in essentially the same form in 2 Samuel 22, in a series of summary chapters about David's life and reign. This song develops out of the singer's personal experience with despair and deliverance, vengeance and victory. At some points the singer seems to be congratulating himself on his purity and righteousness; we may even feel that David has grown too smug with himself. Several aspects of this point should be considered: First of all, verses such as Psalm 18:20,23 should be read in the context of the whole psalm which includes praise to God for what he has done in and through David (verse 32) as well as in his own power (verses 7–15). Second, we are given God's comments on David in several places such as 1 Kings 11:4 and 14:8 which remind us of his keeping of God's commandments. Obviously in the sense of sinlessness, only Jesus Christ was perfect, but the word is often used to indicate wholehearted devotion to God's law.

PSALM 18: READ ALOUD

WHAT DOES IT SAY? WHAT DOES IT MEAN?

Figurative
Language

Tone

Unity

1. In verses 1–3, what picture of God does the singer offer?

   What tone does the exclamation of verse 1 set for the rest of the song?

   In verse 2, what metaphor unifies the picture of God?

   How does verse 3 introduce the specific purpose of this song?

   David's God is loving, strong, and worthy of praise because of his care and constant provision. This poem is a song of love, an overflowing of a grateful heart because of God's acts of deliverance. These acts are described throughout the song; then in verse 49, the singer says, "Therefore . . . . " The expression of love with which the song begins has been given its reasons, making thanks and praise appropriate. But because the nature of God's deliverance has been from military enemies rather than from, say, disease, God is portrayed in military metaphors. If disease had been David's enemy, he might have written of God as a doctor or nurse, a hospital or oxygen tent; instead, God is a fortress, a shield, a high tower, and so on. Deliverance from the enemy is a reason for praise, and so the specific purpose of this song is that praise.

2. In verses 4–6, what is the singer's need and source of help?

Poetic Structure

What poetic patterns does the singer use in these verses to show his condition?

Two references to impending death and one to Sheol (the grave or hell) suggest the singer's fears brought on by threats of his enemies. In complete anguish of spirit he calls on God to save him. The singer knows—because of subsequent deliverance—that his cry had been heard. David uses both parallelism and cause-effect patterns. Verse 5 is a good example of parallelism; verse 6 shows cause ("I called") and effect ("he heard").

Parallelism

Cause-Effect

3. In verses 7–15, how is the singer's deliverance accomplished?

Figurative Language

What do the major figures of speech have in common?

What does the singer mean to suggest by these references to weather and storms?

Throughout this section of the psalm, the language compares the power of God to earthquakes, floods, hailstorms, thunder and lightning, darkness, and winds. God's power collapses the enemy and overwhelms them. Like the fierceness of a storm, there is no withstanding the power of God. David may be referring to a specific instance in which his pursuing enemies were turned back by a flash flood or hailstorm or some other meteorological phenomenon attributed to God's intervention. Or he may simply be using this figurative language as a means of countering the claims of his enemies, that their pagan deities were responsible for weather conditions.

4. In verses 16–19, by what poetic method does the singer reveal his dependence on God?

Poetic Structure

What poetic pattern does he use in verse 18?

David makes no pretense of having delivered himself. In each of these three verses the emphasis is on God in the pronoun *he*. The enemy is too strong for David but not for God, who provides stability in the middle of a torrent rushing by. He also delivers out of the cramped quarters of hiding—as in a cave—and provides a place open and wide enough to enjoy. The word *but* in the middle of verse 18 points to the poetic device called antithesis: The enemy did this, *but* the Lord did that.

Antithesis

5. In verses 20–29, by what right does the singer appear to be applauding himself?

If we were to see this passage as a courtroom scene, with God as Judge, with David and his enemies in a law suit against each other, how might we better understand David's claims?

How does verse 27 help to answer our questions about the singer's apparent boasting?

In verses 28–29, how does the singer

return to his previous expressions of dependence?

As has already been indicated in the Background, this passage may be troublesome to students who find in it an attitude of self-righteousness. Those who know David's story well enough to know his sins as well as his attributes as a man of God may react negatively here. You can point out that David measures himself by an objective standard, namely God's law—"the ways of the Lord," "his decrees" ("statutes," KJV). This places David in the courtroom, as it were, with his enemies and himself to be judged by the Righteous Judge. By contrast, his enemies pervert the law of God. In quite specific terms, the tribes against whom David fought all his life were barbaric idolaters whose worship included human sacrifice, gross sexual promiscuity, and the attributing of good to evil sources. Below the surface appearance of self-righteousness, therefore, lies something less offensive in David's claims. David is not overly proud of his goodness; in fact, he classifies himself (in verse 28) as needing a light in the darkness. In verse 29, he fully attributes his deliverance to God: it has been solely by God's help that he has escaped capture.

6. In verses 30–45, what military turn of events is the singer describing?

In what specific ways has the Lord helped the singer achieve his victory?

Interpretation

Why doesn't the singer offer any mercy to his enemies?

In these verses David's distress and deliverance turn to the routing of his enemies. In verse 37, for instance, we are told this plainly.

By following God's law, David learns God's reliability (verse 30), security (verse 31), and strength (verse 32). The result is given once again in military terms, similar to verse 2: God is a shield and armor, an instructor in the skills of battle, a source of encouragement in combat, making the pursuit of the enemy possible. The singer shows no mercy for, perhaps, these reasons: culturally, it was not the custom of David's time to show mercy to a defeated enemy; historically, sparing the enemy when God had commanded their destruction had been the reason for Saul's disgrace and rejection; theologically, as David says in verse 25, God is merciful to the merciful (KJV), and few of David's enemies would qualify as merciful.

7. In verses 46–50, how does the singer sum up his final praise to God?

   What ongoing hope or promise does the singer claim?

Unlike the gods of his enemies, David's God lives! He alone is worthy of praise because God, not David, is really the King. God has proved himself; *therefore* the singer offers this song of thanksgiving. Furthermore, the singer has assurance that the God of David will be faithful to David's descendants forever. Implicit in this assurance, however, must be the human side to the bargain, which means that David's descendants must also keep God's law.

HOW DOES THIS APPLY TO ME?

1. This psalm speaks of God's power in figurative language describing severe weather. Does God use weather conditions to work his will? (See Job 36:22–33; 37:10–13.) Are earth-

quakes or tornadoes sent by God for specific reasons? What about the statement by Jesus, that God the Father sends rain "on the evil and the good" (Matt. 5:45, NIV)?

2. The Bible and many of our Christian hymns make frequent reference to military figures of speech—"Onward Christian Soldiers," the warfare against sin, and so on. Some Christians find this analogy with war offensive because, they say, Jesus is the Prince of Peace (Isa. 9:6). How do you feel about this use of figurative language to describe the Christian experience? What verses in the Bible make use of the military metaphors (see Ephesians 6, 1 Peter 5:8, et al.)?

3. God saves us not only from physical enemies, but also from sin. How am I appropriating his strength and deliverance in my life?

4.

5.

PUTTING THIS LESSON INTO ACTION

1. If you feel that God has answered prayer and delivered you from some specific danger or illness, write a short psalm in the style of David's songs. Try to use the patterns you have identified as parallelism, antithesis, and cause-effect.

2. One of David's favorite metaphors for God is "my rock." Use a Bible concordance and look up several references to the word *rock* in the Bible. What divine qualities or attributes are being represented in comparing God to a rock? What contemporary comparison might we choose today to describe God?

3. The many vivid metaphors of this psalm lend themselves well to visual illustration. Make a series of posters or cartoons depicting the progress recorded in this psalm, from distress to deliverance to chasing the enemy.

2 Samuel 11, 12; Psalm 51

BACKGROUND

After David moves the capital from Hebron to Jerusalem and constructs his fortress there, he decides to consolidate his power by also changing the location of the Ark of God. Since the Philistines returned it to the Israelites, it had been left at Kiriath-Jearim (see 1 Samuel 4–6). Two remarkable incidents occur during the transfer of the Ark—the death of Uzzah and the transformation of the house belonging to Obed-Edom (2 Samuel 6; see also 1 Chronicles 13:5–14; 15:1–16:3).

The arrival of the Ark in Jerusalem is an occasion for great rejoicing; in the Chronicles account, the narrative quotes Psalm 105:1–15, Psalm 96, and Psalm 106:1,47,48, as having been sung at that time. But it is also a time of bitterness for David because his exuberance offends his first wife Michal, and they quarrel over his dancing.

Second Samuel 7 introduces us to Nathan the prophet, who is an important figure in David's life. David's first recorded encounter with him comes when David proposes building the temple of God. At first Nathan approves; but later the Lord discloses to Nathan that David is not to build the temple—one of his sons will. David accepts this prophecy in goodwill. His prayer in chapter 7:18–29 is one of the great prayers of the Old Testament. You might read this aloud to the class.

As time passes, David goes out to subsequent battles and glorious victories. But during the fighting he recalls his promise to Jonathan and brings to the court the crippled son of Jonathan, Mephibosheth.

All of these incidents serve as important preliminaries to the tragedy of 2 Samuel 11 and 12. David's reign has begun in honor. But his involvement with Bathsheba and the murder of her husband put a blight on David which affects the rest of his life, even though he can experience the forgiveness of those sins.

Psalm 51 is treated as a whole in discussion questions rather than being analyzed in small units. If time is limited, study of this psalm may be omitted, although its importance to the completeness of the story should not be overlooked.

This is not an episode which requires much moralizing for students to understand. Its point is perfectly obvious. Students may or may not feel at ease in discussing this story's details, depending both on their maturity and the atmosphere of mutual respect present in the classroom. Mature students respond best to a frank and unembarrassed discussion. Many of them are familiar with adultery in the lives of their friends and neighbors and as depicted on television.

2 SAMUEL 11, 12; PSALM 51: READ ALOUD

WHAT DOES IT SAY? WHAT DOES IT MEAN?

1. What progression in sinning, from first to last, does this story show?

   When does David's sin begin?

   How much is Bathsheba responsible for her sin?

Sin is both attitude and action; it isn't classifiable, as our legal system would suggest, into misdemeanors and felonies. The consequences of sin may intensify and become more grossly evil, but all these result from the same source. In this story David's sin is covetousness, a violation of the tenth commandment (see Exodus 20:17); eventually, he becomes guilty of adultery and murder as well. It begins, however, not when he first sees the beautiful woman bathing but when he begins to covet her, lusting for her (see Matthew 5:27-28). We are not accountable for the potential sin in any human activity. Accountability begins when we shift from circumstances to thinking about the possibilities within those circumstances. For example, my neighbor purchases an elegant new automobile and parks it in his driveway next door. I have no control over his action, and there may be no way I can avoid seeing the new car day after day. If I can honestly share in the owner's delight without coveting the car for myself, I avoid sin altogether. Seeing somebody else's car is not sin; wanting one like it and being willing to work in a responsible manner to buy such a car is no sin. But wanting the car and wishing I had it and the neighbor didn't is sin. From this first step disaster may result.

Bathsheba is undoubtedly under unusual pressure, having been summoned by the king. Presumably David's message did not outright propose adultery; so she cannot be faulted for obeying her sovereign in coming to his palace. When he does propose adultery, she may still feel pressure, but she becomes responsible like anyone else for the consequences of her actions. Because the narrative gives no indication that she refused or was threatened (as does the story in 2 Samuel 13 regarding Amnon and Tamar), we may assume that Bathsheba was a willing partner.

Plot

2. What is David's scheme?

Why does David summon Uriah as soon as he learns that Bathsheba is pregnant?

David wishes to avoid any consequences of his sin with Bathsheba. If he can make it appear that the child is legitimately Bathsheba's husband's, David can be free of social responsibility. He shows no sign of moral responsibility. So he orders Uriah back from the battlefront, ostensibly to receive a military

report from him. While at ease from the battle, Uriah will undoubtedly enjoy going home
and making love with his wife; thus the baby
can be assumed to be his.

Character   3. What can you tell about Uriah's character?

*Why does he refuse to visit his wife
during his leave from the battle?*

*What is the final frustration to David's
scheme?*

Uriah is not only a dedicated soldier (he had
been one of David's mighty men for a long
time, 1 Chron. 11:41), but also a man of honor
with deep consideration for his fellows. He
may also be perceptive enough to question
the whole matter of his somewhat strange
mission back to Jerusalem. Certainly David
could have learned what little he asked of
Uriah concerning the troops from almost any
messenger. Why is David so solicitous of
Uriah's comfort and well-being—urging him
to go home and freshen up, sending a lavish
gift? But Uriah refuses to take advantage of
any privilege; his comrades-in-arms are still
enduring military hardship; so must he. He
knows that, in going to his own home, he will
yield to his love for his beautiful wife; thus he
disciplines himself by depriving himself of
normal marital relations. Even after David
deliberately intoxicates him, Uriah has too
much will power to yield; instead, he spends
another night with David's servants and
leaves the next morning for the battlefield,
never having spent a moment with his wife.
So remarkable has been his behavior and so
public, nobody will believe Bathsheba's story
that the baby is Uriah's.

4. Why does David order Uriah's death?

Why does David involve Joab in his plot against Uriah?

Connotation

Upon hearing the news of Uriah's death, what does David's message to Joab mean?

David is motivated by pride tainted by frustration. He has tried an easy way out of the responsibility for the unborn child; a noble soldier has refused to cooperate in being the cuckolded husband. So David takes it on himself to reward the husband for his nobility by killing him. At least with Uriah dead, he won't be able to cause a scandal. Joab is David's commander-in-chief, and like David a man of bloody hands (see 2 Samuel 3:22–34). Although David has condemned Joab for committing murder in the past, David is not afraid to reveal his own murderous intentions to his nephew Joab (1 Chron. 2:16–17). He knows that they are two of a kind. When David's orders have been followed and Uriah is dead, David reacts to the news with a pose of anger and remorse that any of his men should have been lost; then he changes his mood and speaks what Joab will interpret as congratulations on a job well done. He also indulges in a cover-up of his crime, speaking platitudinously about the vagaries of war and the fact that you never can tell who is going to be lost in battle.

Parable

5. Explain Nathan's parable.

Application

How does a leader's behavior affect his nation?

What is the initial effect of the parable on David?

When David knows its meaning, how does the parable affect him?

At the end of 2 Samuel 11, David's affair with
Bathsheba appears to be reaching a satisfac-
tory conclusion: she has mourned an appropriate length of time, David has married
Bathsheba, their child has been born. But
David has not counted on God's retribution.
Nathan the prophet (see 2 Samuel 7) arrives
as God's spokesman. Nathan is responding to
a national need, the need to restore honor and
justice to the throne. He sets about his task by
the indirect means of a parable. Students may
not realize that other speakers besides Jesus
of Nazareth told parables; in fact, teaching by
means of parables was common throughout
the ancient world. Like all parables, Nathan's
does not presume to be an exact analogy to
the given situation; a parable "runs along-
side" reality, paralleling it with a searchlight
of truth. In this parable the similarities are
perfectly straightforward. David's reaction is
as expected—an outburst of anger against the
rich man's cruelty and injustice to the poor
man. After Nathan has pointed the finger of
accusation and spoken God's condemnation,
David admits his sin.

6. What punishment from God does Nathan
   predict?

   *How does David react during his son's
   illness and after the child's death?*

   *Why does God punish David through
   the child's death instead of by taking
   David's life?*

Any question about God's justice must be approached in the most tentative terms. As
human beings, we simply do not comprehend
God's ways. David reacts to the parable by
exclaiming that the rich man should die for
taking the poor man's lamb. But God's

punishment is even more severe than simply taking David's life. Instead, he causes David to suffer for the rest of his life—first, the death of the infant; then the wretched behavior of Amnon with Tamar; the disgrace of Absalom's conduct with David's harem; then Absalom's death. All his life David must bear the knowledge of the consequences of his sin. During the child's illness David fasts and prays in prostration, hoping for a reprieve from God's judgment; but when the child has died, David becomes resigned to what God will do to him. His hope remains sure: he will be rejoined with the child in the life-after-death. David's statement in 2 Samuel 12:23 gives an indication of Old Testament beliefs about this life which is not given an extended treatment until the New Testament.

Word Choices

7. Psalm 51 is David's prayer for forgiveness. What specific words and phrases throughout this psalm help to convey David's sense of guilt and shame? What are the steps toward forgiveness which David takes in this psalm?

Tone

Parallelism

Figurative Language

This psalm should be read aloud with careful attention to the desperation inherent in its tone. Consider the parallelism in the petitions and in the foreseen results. The speaker is at the end of his rope. He pleads for mercy to blot out his sins, so great a laundry bleach would be necessary to rid his clothes of the stain. He acknowledges the extent of his sin: it is ultimately against God. He petitions for a new purity of heart and the right spirit of humility, since pride was the source of his sin. He remembers that God's Spirit had left Saul, so he prays that the Holy Spirit will stay with him. He asks to be forgiven for the guilt

of Uriah's murder. Specific steps toward forgiveness may be pointed out as *recognition of
sin* and *need for redemption* followed by
confession and *petition for renewal and restoration.* Other similar terms may be substi-
tuted.

8. What results will follow from this confession and repentance?

David's joy will be restored and other sinners
will also return to God as they hear David
praise God for his ways. "A broken and contrite heart" and "righteous sacrifices" will
please God. David's restoration will be followed by the building up of Jerusalem as
well. Consider the differences caused by the
fact that Saul never did repent while David
did.

HOW DOES THIS APPLY TO ME?

1. Someone has said concerning temptation and sin, "We're not
   to blame for the birds that fly overhead, only for those that
   nest in our hair." What does this old adage mean?
2. David's sin had continuing effects even after his forgiveness.
   What kinds of effects can be expected after sins committed
   by people in the age group of those in your class—perhaps
   drunkenness, drug addiction, cheating, stealing, sexual im-
   morality, gluttony, disobedience to parents, etc.?
3. Pride is seen as the source of all sin. What is pride? With
   sexual sin, the pride relates to the desire to control others by
   the appeal of our bodies. How does this sinful pride differ
   from love?
4. Many people no longer feel that sexual relations before marriage or outside of marriage are wrong. What is the basis for
   Christian teaching on this subject? What part does moral responsibility play? Are there situations where a person's
   moral guilt for a situation might differ from his legal guilt?
   Discuss some examples.

5.

6.

PUTTING THIS LESSON INTO ACTION

1. Supposing you were given Nathan's responsibility to confront the king with his sin. Write a parable or fable by which
to convict David of his guilt.
2. Because of the cultural context, Bathsheba is entirely in the
background of this story, and there is no discussion of abortion. Among other reasons, abortions were often dangerous
and the birth of a child was welcomed as a blessing from
God. Rewrite this episode from a twentieth century point of
view, which would consider Bathsheba's situation and
the ethical possibilities. Consider Christian perspectives
on abortion, including *Whatever Happened to the Human
Race?* by Francis A. Schaeffer and C. Everett Koop (Old
Tappan, N.J.: Revell, 1979).
3. Every individual needs forgiveness for some offense against
God, whether it be as notorious as David's sin or as common
as selfishness and lying. Write out a personal prayer asking
for forgiveness. You will not have to show it to anybody.
4. Find out what Christians in your area are doing to help
unwed mothers, in adoption agencies, shelters, and educational and vocational assistance programs. Are these helps
available through individual people or through institutions?

LESSON 10

Psalm 3; 2 Samuel 18:1–19:8

BACKGROUND

As part of God's judgment against David for his sin with Bathsheba, Nathan the prophet foretells trouble within David's family and public scandal. This prophecy is not long in waiting to be fulfilled.

In 2 Samuel 13–18, the sons of David engage in violent and treacherous acts that bring trouble and shame to themselves and others and that attempt to overthrow the king himself. In these same chapters we can begin to glimpse something of David's weakness as a father: in the greatness of his affection for his sons he appears to have lacked the loving hand of discipline. Punishments of death were prescribed in the law for unlawful sexual relations and for rebellious sons.

The trouble begins with Amnon's sexual attack on his half-sister Tamar (2 Sam. 13). Her brother Absalom avenges his sister by killing Amnon; but for all this evildoing, David does nothing but weep bitterly.

In 2 Samuel 14–17, Absalom begins to capitalize on his father's weakness and strikes out against David in rebellion. Because of his great physical beauty and personal charm—what politicians today call "charisma"—Absalom is able to win over the people of Israel, so that King David has to flee for his life; Absalom is actually crowned, and David is cursed by his own people as a man of blood unworthy to be king. To dramatize his treachery against his father, Absalom engages in a sexual orgy with David's harem—a final act of disrespect.

This is the state of affairs when David writes the words of Psalm 3, a psalm beginning in despondency and ending in affirmation of deliverance. Yet the circumstances through which that deliverance would be achieved would bring to David even greater sorrows. His failure as a father almost exceeds his accomplishments as a warrior and king.

But even in the depths of personal failure, David does not forget to seek help and sustaining strength from God; furthermore, God does not desert him, in spite of his inability to control his family. Thus, from first to last, the story of David remains a very human story, one from which most of us should gain a good deal of comfort.

Regarding the two passages under study in this lesson: Both Psalm 3 and 2 Samuel 18 are brief enough to be studied as whole pieces of literature. Although there are several natural divisions, the questions in this lesson are aimed at looking at the whole psalm or narrative, rather than at individual verses or incidents. In every case the most complete responses will be generated by close examination of the text; but that close study is only for the purpose of achieving a larger perspective. These questions are not developmental: question 2 does not necessarily grow out of an acceptable response to question 1. The teacher should select one of these questions and build the discussion around it.

PSALM 3: READ ALOUD

WHAT DOES IT SAY? WHAT DOES IT MEAN?

Structure

1. Divide the psalm into its main parts. Give a subtitle or theme to each part.

The singer begins with an exclamation that probably refers to the number of enemies amassed by his rebellious son Absalom. However, sheer numbers are not as menacing as is the particular nature of these enemies. Never before has David faced his own son in battle. With his people defecting from him and his crown usurped, David is the subject of dire negative predictions. So verses 1 and 2 constitute a pessimistic opening section in this song. Section two, however, swings on the hinging word *but*. All attention is turned away from the enemies and the prophets of doom to look instead at the Lord and his strength. This middle section of the song offers the reasons for hope in verses 3–6. Verses 7 and 8 conclude the song with a challenge to God and an ascription of praise for the victory yet to be accomplished. Students will differ in their means of expression, but they should not vary widely from the natural structure of the psalm, as indicated by its language.

Tone

2. How does the tone in this song change from one emotional level to another?

In verse 1, the initial exclamation of alarm indicates a tone of fear. In verse 3, the singer finds cause for hope in the fact of God's presence and protection. By verse 5, the singer is no longer afraid of vast numbers of enemies. In verse 7, the singer is cheering on his champion, and by verse 8, the tone anticipates total victory.

3. Why is it especially important to the singer in this circumstance that God should be victorious?

Several factors, in and out of the song, make God's victory and David's vindication important. In the psalm, students should be able to comment on the derision of the scoffers in verse 2. In verse 3, the singer refers to his head being raised up, which means that he is at present in an ashamed, head-hanging posture. The cause of his shame is the larger context of this psalm, specifically Absalom's rebellion and the outrage he has committed in David's harem. Furthermore, if David is "the Lord's anointed," it must be proved in God's deliverance this time; or else the threat of usurpation will stalk any king of Israel. Lastly, the singer makes it clear that his entire trust is unreservedly in God, who is to receive all the praise for the victory. This is the singer's challenge to his divine champion.

2 SAMUEL 18:1–19:8: READ ALOUD

WHAT DOES IT SAY? WHAT DOES IT MEAN?

1. How does the narrator show David's great love for Absalom throughout this story?

   Should the king put his own son ahead of the nation?

From the outset of Absalom's *coup d'état,* David has shown no desire to fight with him over the kingdom. He leaves Jerusalem rather than allow Absalom to become guilty of the death of innocent people. He weeps as he goes, and we may infer that his mixed emotions include pain over Absalom's defection. In this chapter, David announces his intention to fight but is easily persuaded not to join the battle; instead, he pleads for his men to treat Absalom gently—surely a strange request concerning a rebel. Everyone in David's fighting force understands the king's order, which is why the man who informs Joab of Absalom's whereabouts declines to kill Absalom himself. When the two messengers arrive before David, both speak indirectly; neither can bring himself to say outright that Absalom is dead. David passes over the news of the battle and asks only about his son. He needs no direct message, and his reaction is deepest grief. The denouement of the episode is found in 2 Samuel 19:1–8.

Conflict

2. How does the narrator develop some of the natural conflicts in this story?

The conflicts are between father and son; king and usurper; David the mighty warrior and David the lenient father; the king's orders and Joab's sense of military justice; two messengers of victory and the question they refuse to answer; victory in battle and the loss of a son. Students may find other conflicts as well. Such conflicts are the natural result of disorder resulting from rebellion, which inverts the proper order and overturns authority.

Character

3. How do you account for the fact that David's temperament seems different in this story from earlier stories?

Obviously David finds himself in a situation far different from any he has ever faced before. Being pursued by Saul generated a different kind of anxiety from what he feels fleeing from his own son. He is torn by deep feelings of paternal love; at the same time, he has a responsibility as "the Lord's anointed" to his kingdom. He is subdued, reluctant to fight with both fists; in 2 Samuel 15:25–26, he seems quite resigned to the possibility that the Lord intends to displace him with Absalom. We should perhaps infer from this text that, if David had found Absalom in the forest, he would have cut his hair free and welcomed him back to Jerusalem. In short, David has been overwhelmed by the emotional shock of having his son rebel against him. We need to remember how unhappy David's family life has been: his first wife Michal was taken from him, then restored but not to happiness and mutual respect; his next six wives each bore him a son, two of whom (Amnon and Absalom) have already died dishonorably; his eighth wife Bathsheba bore a son who also died. As David grows older and his sorrows increase, he seems to become much less exuberant and impetuous.

HOW DOES THIS APPLY TO ME?

1. One of David's sons, the wise King Solomon, said, "Train a child in the way he should go" (Prov. 22:6, NIV). What appears to have been his father David's philosophy of child-rearing? Investigate not only verses such as 1 Kings 1:5,6 but also David's prayers for and advice for Solomon in 1 Chronicles 28:9–10,20; 29:19. You should also look for verses about parental responsibility in Proverbs and in the law of Moses. What is your philosophy on how children should be disciplined?
2. Why do young people rebel against governmental authority? What are your responsibilities to your political leaders?
3. Knowing how to deliver a message, particularly an unhappy message, requires a good deal of common sense and tact. It also requires a person to know something about the one to whom he gives the message. How would you deliver the following messages?
   a. tell your parents that you have just received a failing grade on a major examination
   b. tell your best friend that your family is moving 1000 miles away
   c. tell your teacher that you cheated on the last quiz
   d. tell a classmate that she has not been chosen for the cheerleading squad
   e. tell your wife or husband that you've had a collision and totally wrecked the car
   f. tell a young child that one of his parents is seriously ill and may not survive

4.

5.

PUTTING THIS LESSON INTO ACTION

1. Survey some current Christian periodicals to discover what kinds of political and family issues are under consideration.
2. Absalom's rebellion against David led to a civil war. What

happens when parents and their children are on different sides of an issue? Are there ways to resolve the problem? Discuss.

3. Look into the biblical accounts of the relationship between David and his nephew Joab.

4. If your students are interested in studying further aspects of David's life and writings, encourage the use of a concordance. In addition to more episodes in the historical books and more psalms written by him, there are also references in the Prophets and in many New Testament books as well.

Unit Test

This test is designed to be a culminating learning experience in the study of David's life and selected psalms. The test may be used to evaluate two dimensions of learning: (1) mastery of the content and (2) mastery of skills developed throughout this unit.

Content questions are generally useful in classes in which students are not yet confident of their ability to use the analytical method of study. Content questions are generally classified as "either/or" problems: either the student knows the right answer or he does not. Skills questions demand a more mature ability to read and reason because they call for the full range of analytical and interpretive reading.

A test which fails to challenge or which exceeds the ability of all but the most capable students has not provided a learning experience for the class. The teacher may be well advised to construct a test suitable to the given students' needs, using problems from both parts of the test provided, as those problems seem appropriate.

Some teachers may elect to offer both tests on consecutive days. In this instance the test of content might serve as a review of the unit's material, with the test of skills serving to evaluate the deeper levels of learning.

MASTERY TEST OF CONTENT

IDENTIFICATION MATCH-UPS

Write the proper name identifying the persons or places listed below. Use the list at the right as your source. (*ANSWERS* are in parentheses).

1. Israel's first king *(SAUL)*
2. Philistine king *(ACHISH)*
3. Giant killed by David *(GOLIATH)*

Jesse
Vale of Elah
Nathan

4. David and Bathsheba's second son
   (SOLOMON)
5. David's commander *(JOAB)*
6. Israel's perennial enemies
   (PHILISTINES)
7. David's unlawful wife *(BATHSHEBA)*
8. Where Saul consulted the witch
   (ENDOR)
9. Prophet who exposed David's sin
   (NATHAN)
10. David's first capital city *(HEBRON)*
11. Saul's commander *(ABNER)*
12. David's birthplace *(BETHLEHEM)*
13. Prophet who anointed David
    (SAMUEL)
14. Saul's eldest son, David's friend
    (JONATHAN)
15. Saul's daughter, David's wife
    (MICHAL)
16. David's third son who rebelled
    (ABSALOM)
17. David's second capital city
    (JERUSALEM)
18. Bathsheba's husband *(URIAH)*
19. David's eldest brother *(ELIAB)*
20. David's father *(JESSE)*

Hebron
Eliab
Jerusalem
Merab
Absalom
Bethlehem
Jonathan
Shiloh
Endor
Bathsheba
Philistines
Amnon
Gath
Carmel
Abigail
Joab
Goliath
Solomon
Achish
Saul
Uriah
Michal
Samuel
Abner
Abinadab

MULTIPLE CHOICE

In each problem choose the response that most satisfactorily
completes the statement.

1. God told Samuel to reject Eliab because
   A. he was too tall
   B. he was too old
   C. God does not choose on the basis of appearances
   D. he was married
2. David volunteered to fight Goliath because he was
   A. a show-off who wanted to humiliate his brothers

    B. angry that Goliath's blasphemy had gone on for forty days

    C. eager for promotion in Saul's army

    D. willing to risk his life to win Saul's reward

3. Saul became jealous of David after

    A. David refused to wear Saul's armor

    B. Jonathan gave David his cloak and sword

    C. David married Michal

    D. the women sang a victory song honoring David more than Saul

4. Jonathan let David know whether or not he was safe by

    A. standing by a tall rock

    B. instructing his servant where to find the arrows

    C. breaking his arrows in their quiver

    D. bending his bow until it broke

5. David refused to harm Saul in the cave because

    A. Saul was unarmed

    B. David preferred to make a fool of Saul

    C. Saul was still "the Lord's anointed"

    D. David wasn't sure that Saul was unarmed

6. The witch whom Saul consulted recognized Saul

    A. as soon as Samuel presented himself to her

    B. because she saw his crown under his disguise

    C. when he fell down at her feet

    D. when Samuel foretold Saul's death

7. David's sin with Bathsheba began when he

    A. first saw her taking a bath

    B. coveted her for himself

    C. committed adultery with her

    D. tried to cover-up his sin by sending Uriah home

8. David's prayer for forgiveness

    A. asks God to spare the dying baby's life

    B. does not include any reference to Uriah's murder

    C. uses several metaphors of cleansing

    D. blames Bathsheba for seducing him

(ANSWERS: 1–C, 2–B, 3–D, 4–B, 5–C, 6–A, 7–B, 8–C)

MEMORIZATION

Write or recite from memory one of the psalms you have learned during this unit of study.

SHORT ANSWERS

Fill in the blanks in each statement with a response which completes the sentence reasonably.

1. David's psalms often reflect his military experience, as when he compares God to a(n) _____ or a(n) _____.

2. In Psalm 18, David speaks of God's power manifest through weather conditions, as in a(n) _____ or a(n) _____.

3. In Psalm 23, the speaker is not afraid in the presence of death because _____.

4. In Psalm 34, David uses a poetic pattern called _____ when he writes, "I will extol the Lord at all times; his praise will always be on my lips."

5. When David writes in Psalm 57:1, "I will take refuge in the shadow of your wings," he is using a metaphor to compare God to _____.

6. In Psalm 51, David says that God isn't interested in sacrifices of burning animals until after _____.

(ANSWERS: 1–*sword, shield, buckler, tower, fortress, and so on*; 2–*earthquake, flood, hailstorm, thunderstorm, and so on*; 3–*God himself is present*; 4–*parallelism*; 5–*a protective mother hen*; 6–*complete repentance*)

MASTERY TEST OF SKILLS

A. Read 2 Samuel 23:1–4 and write a brief answer to each of the following questions.
  1. How many different ways does David identify himself? What is distinctive about each identification?
  2. Who is the source or inspiration of David's songs?
  3. What are God's qualifications for his anointed king?
  4. What lesson can a modern reader learn from this text?

B. Read 2 Samuel 9:1-13. After carefully considering the story, write a brief essay in which you explain:
   1. why this incident is necessary in the story of David;
   2. what it contributes to our fuller understanding of David's character;
   3. what it illustrates about godliness and responsibility.
C. Read 1 Kings 1:6. On the basis of what you know about David's life—as a son in Jesse's household and as a husband and father in his own household—write an essay in which you discuss David's experience with his own children. Why did he succeed as a father? Why did he fail? What can we learn from David's experience?
D. In both the narratives and the psalms it appears evident that David knew a good deal about nature and life in the outdoors at firsthand. As a shepherd, he kept his flock in an outdoor fold; as a fugitive from Saul, as a soldier and king, he was often in caves or in the open fields. Write an essay in which you describe David's relationship with God through nature.

HELPFUL BOOKS

Aharoni, Yohanan and Michael Avi-Yonah. *The Macmillan Bible Atlas.* New York: Macmillan, 1968.

Maps are given in scriptural order (more than thirty maps relate to Samuel, Saul, David, and Jonathan). There is some discussion of events, but this is primarily a book of maps. For early parts of the Bible, chronological decisions sometimes differ from conservative views. A useful feature, however, is a chronological table paralleling events in Palestine with those in Egypt, other parts of the Near East, and eventually the West as well.

Alden, Robert. *Psalms.* 3 vols. Chicago: Moody, 1974–76.

Brief paperback volumes endeavor to combine piety and scholarship, suggesting word meanings, psalm division, structural techniques, including chiasmus.

Alexander, David and Patricia Alexander, eds. *Eerdmans' Handbook to the Bible.* Grand Rapids: Eerdmans, 1973.

Sections deal with the Bible in its overall environment as well as discussion of plants, animals, weights, seasons. Directories of themes, nationalities, subjects, events, and prayers in the Bible and essays on many topics are accompanied by excellent photographs and charts. A discussion of poetic techniques and of the Book of Psalms (including a list of those connected with David), and maps of the military actions of Saul and David are helpful.

Anderson, Stanley E. *Our Dependable Bible.* Grand Rapids: Baker, 1960.

This work provides an easily read defense of the Scriptures as reliable, considering archeology, prophecies, the testimony of Christ, the Bible's own claims. It presents a list of quotations from people with confidence in the Scriptures and suggests possible explanations for problem areas.

Baly, Denis. *The Geography of the Bible.* New York: Harper, 1957.

Maps and photographs are accompanied by discussion of various sections of Palestine, with many references to the political implications of a geographic feature or location. Extensive index, Scripture index, bibliography, and glossary of geologic terms.

Book of Psalms for Singing. Pittsburgh: The Board of Education and Publication, Reformed Presbyterian Church of North America, 1973.

Most of the Psalms are set to one or more familiar tunes so that a class will have little trouble singing them. Singing Psalms aids in the appreciation of the poem as a whole. These translations are good and the pages are clearly readable.

Crockett, William Day. *A Harmony of the Books of Samuel, Kings, and Chronicles.* Grand Rapids: Baker, 1964 reprint.

Parallel columns help the reader to compare Scripture passages in more than one book that refer to the same event, especially so that the viewpoint of Chronicles can be understood in relation to the others.

Edersheim, Alfred. *The Life and Times of Jesus the Messiah.* Grand Rapids: Eerdmans, 1972 reprint.

This work represents excellent New Testament background material, considering the Jewish world in the time of Christ, with extensive references to the Jewish Targums, giving views on feasts and customs.

Free, Joseph. *Archaeology and Biblical History.* 5th ed. Wheaton: Scripture Press, 1956.

An emphasis on facets of history which are illuminated through artifacts and other discoveries is given. For example, there is a section on Davidic music.

Gaebelein, Frank E. *Exploring the Bible.* New York: Harper, 1929.

An overall discussion surveys how we got our Bible, how to study the Bible, how the Bible is organized. It also gives a presentation of God's promises or covenants, including the Davidic Covenant.

_____. *The Christian Use of the Bible.* Chicago: Moody, 1946.

Here Gaebelein gives an apologetic for reading the Bible: it is profitable for doctrine, reproof, correction, instruction in righteousness. The Holy Spirit illuminates, but we must read.

Holman, C. Hugh. *A Handbook to Literature.* 3rd ed. Indianapolis: Odyssey, 1972.

Literary terms and genres are explained, with illustrations. Discussions of parallelism, poetry, parable, point of view, narrative, etc., are helpful for Bible study.

Howkins, Kenneth G. *The Challenge of Religious Studies.* London: Tyndale Press, 1972.

Religious Education is a compulsory course in British schools. How-kins is aware that many teachers of Religious Education may be in-fluenced by liberal and even atheistic critics of the Bible. He argues for the authenticity of the Scriptures in a strongly reasoned case.

Lockerbie, D. Bruce. *Patriarchs and Prophets: Literature from the Old Testament.* New York: Holt, Rinehart and Winston, 1969.

One of the first textbooks available for public school courses in "the Bible as literature," this book introduces students to four types of Old Testament literature: epic, narrative, poetry, and prophecy. Study materials and questions on the text are included.

——————————. *The Cosmic Center.* Grand Rapids: Eerdmans, 1977.

Secularism is at war with Christian supernaturalism and the claim that Jesus Christ is Lord. Materialism, behaviorism, humanism, hedonism, and nihilism are some of the secular substitutes for the Lordship of Christ. But at the center of the cosmos stands the Christ of Colossians 1 and 2. This book helps a Bible teacher see im-mediately the day-to-day implications of what Scripture teaches and secularism denies.

——————————. *The Liberating Word: Art and the Mystery of the Gospel.* Chapters 1–4. Grand Rapids: Eerdmans, 1974.

Early chapters deal with "making known the mystery of the Gospel" in a verbal manner, whether oral or written. Of special interest to Bible teachers will be the author's concept of "a sanctified imagina-tion" and the relationship between myth and truth.

May, Herbert G. *Oxford Bible Atlas.* 2nd ed. New York: Oxford, 1974.

This work emphasizes general maps for a time period, rather than individual episodes. Physical and political features are often com-bined; maps of rainfall and vegetation areas are useful. Good photos and extensive commentary are included.

Mickelson, A. Berkeley. *Interpreting the Bible.* Grand Rapids: Eerdmans, 1963.

Under general hermeneutics, chapters are devoted to context, lan-guage, and history and culture. Special hermeneutics topics include figures of speech, typology, symbols, prophecy, description, poetry, doctrine, and devotion. Examples from Scripture form an integral part of the discussion.

Miller, Madeleine S. and J. Lane Miller. *Harper's Bible Dictionary.* 8th ed. New York: Harper and Row, 1973.

Articles on peoples, places, objects, together with photographs and maps are useful for reference. However, the viewpoint on authorship of the Psalms is less conservative than that taken in this book, as is also the case with other points.

Nave's Topical Bible. Orville J. Nave, ed. Chicago: Moody, 1921.

Subjects of the Bible are arranged by topics and often subdivided with a phrase to indicate the content of a particular passage. Many verses are given in full. Under "David," events in David's life are listed, together with a probable time of writing each of his psalms. After the biography, more than a dozen other features of the Bible's treatment of him are listed. A Scripture index gives ideas of subjects which are treated in a given passage which could then lead to other verses on the same subject.

Perrine, Laurence. *Sound and Sense: An Introduction to Poetry.* 3rd ed. New York: Harcourt, Brace, Jovanovich, 1969.

The bestselling textbook on how to read and understand poetry. Perrine treats his reader to the process of reading a poem without ever sacrificing the art behind the writing of the poem. His methods of analysis and synthesis are a model of teaching more Bible teachers should follow!

Pfeiffer, Charles F. *Baker's Bible Atlas.* Grand Rapids: Baker, 1961.

Hammond color maps and pictures illuminate a lengthy text discussing individual places and Scripture references where they are mentioned. An interesting feature focuses on David's foreign conquests.

Pfeiffer, Charles F. and Howard F. Vos. *The Wycliffe Historical Geography of Bible Lands.* Chicago: Moody, 1967.

This volume includes all the Bible lands, not just Palestine, giving hundreds of pictures and line maps as well as paying attention to the unfolding of history in these lands. Specific references to the relationship between an historical event and the biblical text are made. Each chapter has footnotes and a bibliography.

Ramm, Bernard. *Protestant Biblical Interpretation.* 3rd ed., rev. Grand Rapids: Baker, 1970.

Ramm first surveys historical schools of interpretation. His own emphases focus on the normal use of words, considering parallel passages, figures of speech, and cultural backgrounds, and on doctrinal and devotional use of the Bible—examples and promises, types, prophecy, and parables among others.

Ryken, Leland. *The Literature of the Bible.* Grand Rapids: Zondervan, 1974.

A thoroughgoing examination of the Bible from the vantage of a literary critic—someone who knows literary forms and the value of understanding these conventions as an aid to understanding the Bible.

Severy, Merle. *Everyday Life in Bible Times.* n.p.: National Geographic Society, 1967.

Beautiful color photographs of people, places, and artifacts are accompanied by discussion of how archeological work is done and good narration of how specific explorations took place. Paintings done by staff artists and by classical painters such as Rembrandt and Raphael help the reader to understand a whole scene.

Sterrett, T. Norton. *How to Understand Your Bible.* rev. ed. Downers Grove, Ill.: InterVarsity, 1974.

Sterrett surveys basic principles of interpretation, with attention to words, grammar, background, figures of speech, symbols, types, parables, allegories, Hebrew idioms, prophecy, and the relationship of the Old and New Testaments.

Strong, James. *Exhaustive Concordance of the Bible.* New York: Abingdon-Cokesbury, 1894.

This verbal index to the Scriptures lists all the verses containing a particular English word, regardless of the Hebrew or Greek. A numerical key to these original words is given which leads to brief dictionaries giving the words in the original language and in transliteration, together with pronunciation and meaning.

Tenney, Merrill C. *The Zondervan Pictorial Bible Dictionary.* Grand Rapids: Zondervan, 1969.

This one-volume handy reference tool gives brief articles on people, places, objects, and events mentioned in the Bible. There are some black and white photographs and maps of the kingdoms of Saul and David.

_____. *The Zondervan Pictorial Encyclopedia of the Bible.* 5 vols. Grand Rapids: Zondervan, 1975.

The article on "David" includes a genealogical chart and a discussion of David in the prophetic books and in the New Testament. "Samuel, 1 & 2" comments on the narrative order and discusses some of the problems raised by the text. "Psalms" considers authorship, compilation, subject matter, and musical characteristics. Long articles have bibliographic lists. (There is no overall index and cross references are often lacking, so use your imagination to find an appropriate article, especially on topical studies.)

Trueblood, Elton. *The Humor of Christ.* New York: Harper and Row, 1964.

With grace and careful fidelity to the Scriptures, Dr. Trueblood shows how our customary somber reading of the Gospels misses the element of humor in the discourses and teaching of Jesus. He reveals how irony, absurdity, and even sarcasm are integral to Christ's presentation of his message. A most important book for anyone who wishes to understand the Gospels better.

Wood, Leon. *A Survey of Israel's History.* Grand Rapids: Zondervan, 1970.

Maps and geographic discussion supplement the historical text. The sections on Saul and David are particularly helpful in suggesting chronological relationships of the events in their lives. Good bibliography, index, and Scripture index.

Young, Robert. *Analytical Concordance to the Bible.* 22nd American Ed. Revised. Grand Rapids: Eerdmans, 1955.

This concordance lists words in English word order, with references subdivided according to whatever Hebrew, Chaldee, or Greek words were in the original text. Phrases are also grouped together. For instance, there are 33 different words translated "taken"; other phrases include "to have taken away," "being taken," "taken down," and "thing that was taken down."

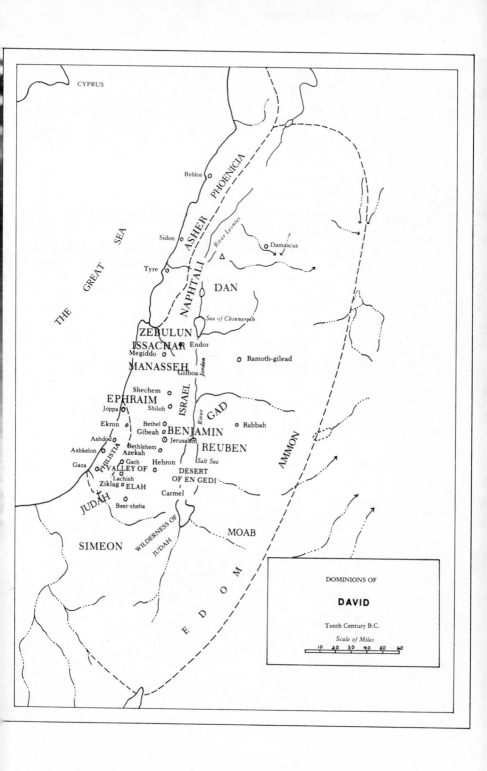

CYPRUS

Byblos

PHOENICIA

ASHER

River Leontes

Sidon

Damascus

Tyre

NAPHTALI

DAN

THE GREAT SEA

Sea of Chinnereth

ZEBULUN

ISSACHAR   Endor

Megiddo

MANASSEH

Gilboa

Ramoth-gilead

Shechem

ISRAEL

GAD

EPHRAIM

Shiloh

River Jordan

Joppa

Ekron   Bethel

Gibeah   BENJAMIN   Rabbah

Ashdod   Jerusalem

Ashkelon   Bethlehem   REUBEN

PHILISTIA   Azekah

AMMON

Gaza   Gath   Hebron

VALLEY OF   Salt Sea

Ziklag   Lachish   DESERT

ELAH   OF EN GEDI

JUDAH   Carmel

Beer-sheba

MOAB

SIMEON   WILDERNESS OF JUDAH

E D O M

DOMINIONS OF

DAVID

Tenth Century B.C.

Scale of Miles

10   20   30   40   50   60

D. Bruce Lockerbie is Dean of Faculty at The Stony Brook School, where he has also served as Chairman of the English Department and the Fine Arts Department. He is the author of more than 500 essays, reviews, and articles, and the co-author or general editor of 20 textbooks. He has also authored books on biography, education, literary criticism, and popular theology, such as *The Way They Should Go, The Liberating Word, The Apostles' Creed,* and *The Cosmic Center.* Mr. Lockerbie is a frequent guest lecturer at Christian schools and colleges and educational conventions.

So you've just received next term's teaching assignment. To your surprise, you find your teaching load includes a class in seventh grade Bible. Of course, you're a Christian, you're glad for this opportunity. You've read and studied the Bible—maybe in Sunday school, maybe in small groups, maybe even in college or Bible institute. But you've never had formal preparation for teaching the Bible in school. Where do you start? How do you teach the Bible to teenagers?

The place to start is by recognizing that the Bible is a book—granted a special book with special authority from a special source. But it is still a *book* made up of words, sentences, paragraphs or stanzas; it is marked off by commas, periods, question marks. In other words, the Bible is a collection of writings or literature. As such, the Bible must be *read* to be comprehended. It must be read using those same powers of intellect and reason with which we seek to read and understand any other literature.

One of the best methods for teaching the Bible is by question and answer. By this method, both teacher and students together read the text open before them and examine it by asking questions, starting at an elementary level and developing an increasingly comprehensive scope to these questions. Each question leads to a variety of responses intended to teach, first, what the text says; then, what it means; finally, how its truth-principles apply to readers today.

4.95